THE ART OF
TABLESCAPING

THE ART OF TABLESCAPING

DECK OUT

YOUR TABLE

WITH THE

QUEEN OF THEME

BUGSY DRAKE

FOREWORD BY CAPTAIN SANDY YAWN

FLASH POINT

FLASH POINT

Published by Flashpoint Books, Seattle, WA
www.flashpointbooks.com

Produced by Girl Friday Productions

Design: Rachel Marek
Photo research: Micah Schmidt
Editorial: Emilie Sandoz-Voyer
Production editorial: Dave Valencia
Project management: Leah Tracosas Jenness

All photos © Alexa Merico except as noted below.

© Daniel Zuliani: front cover; pages 2, 224

© Bugsy Drake: pages 12–18, 26 (left), 27, 28 (middle), 30–31 (bottom left), 32 (bottom), 38 (top, middle), 39, 40 (bottom), 43 (top right), 48 (top), 49 (bottom), 54–57, 58 (bottom), 62 (top), 63, 64–65 (top, bottom left, bottom middle), 70 (bottom), 71, 73 (bottom left), 212–13, 216 (bottom), 217, 222, 224

ISBN (hardcover): 978-1-7348802-2-9

First edition

FOR CHRIS, THE AMAZING
MAN WHO INSPIRED MY DREAM OF
THEME! THANK YOU FOR TEACHING
ME TO LIVE LIFE TO THE FULLEST AND
TO ALWAYS FOLLOW MY PASSION!

WITH LOVE,
BUGS

CONTENTS

FOREWORD

Bugsy is the true queen of tablescapes. Having worked with her, I can say that witnessing her tablescapes is every captain's dream. They are a true extension of her passion in providing incredible, top-of-the-line guest experiences.

Yachts are not built to hold piles and piles of decorations, but Bugsy's creativity eliminates that need. From simple lunches to last-minute parties, Bugsy exceeds my expectations. I always think, "OK, well, that's got to be the biggest, the best, the most incredible tablescape she can do"—but then she blows me away again with her unique creativity.

I'm blessed to routinely work with crews of people who love what they do, and it shows. When someone loves what they do, it pours into their passions. It comes from their soul.

This book represents Bugsy's creativity, uniqueness, and positive energy. I'm honored to be a part of it, and I'm thrilled that people beyond our charters finally get to learn from the Bugsy I know and respect—the best of the best, and the queen of theme.

CAPTAIN SANDY YAWN

HOWZIT?!

I'm Bugsy. If you've seen me on *Below Deck Mediterranean,* you already know a few things about me: I'm from South Africa; I can talk to anyone; I adore anything glam—especially OTT hair clips (for you Americans, those are barrettes); and I'm known for my love of tablescaping.

What you may not know about me is that I come by my affinity for hospitality naturally. Until I was ten years old, I lived in a little town called Linbro Park in Johannesburg, South Africa. My ever-creative mum ran an incredible farmyard there as a children's party venue, which eventually developed into a multifunction event space. Later, we moved to Ballito, a small coastal town where my family still lives today. After we kids moved away, my mother turned our family home into a boutique B&B and wedding venue. While the jump from South Africa to the open sea might seem like a surprising life path, that early experience gave me a love of meeting new people and providing them with memories for a lifetime. As a child I also spent time visiting the sea and going on safari, and that inspired my passion for travel and being on the water. So, not so surprising after all!

In combination, all of these experiences and interests led to my chief stewardess superpower: creating the most luxe, most over-the-top, extraordinary tablescapes on land or sea!

If you don't know me from *Below Deck,* I'll take a brief pause right here because you might be wondering what on earth I'm talking about. *What in the heck is a tablescape?* In its simplest form, a tablescape is a table setting—but really it's so much more. It's the essence of your evening, the theme around which your menu, drinks, lighting, attire, and especially your conversation can revolve. A tablescape is the story you are telling, and it's the journey you and your guests are taking. It's a way to transform a simple meal into a lifetime memory. If I sound hyperbolic, forgive me, but I am really and truly passionate about the power of the tablescape.

FINDING MY WAY TO TABLESCAPING

My own journey into yachting and tablescaping was a pleasant accident. A friend suggested I work on a yacht for a season to earn some travel money before I got into the "real" working world, but I fell in love with the experience immediately. My first yachting

job was on an eighty-meter yacht that traveled between the Caribbean and the Mediterranean. I was fortunate to be part of an awesome twenty-one-person crew. We hosted a lot of theme parties on the boat. It really opened my eyes to this world of entertainment and experience-making for the guests.

In that first job I was a junior stewardess, really a junior-junior! I was pretty much kicked into the laundry and cabins for the entire first year. But I quickly realized there were ways I could create a totally cool experience for the guests even from there. I asked my chief stew if I could

write nice little notes and put them beside our guests' beds. When they went to sleep at night the notes would be a small reminder of their incredible day by including a reference to an activity they had enjoyed. Using a small part of my creative flair and reminding them of special experiences brought joy for me to something as mundane as turndowns in a cabin.

It was on that same yacht that I had my first professional tablescaping experience—and it didn't go according to plan. My chief stew asked me to try my hand at creating a tablescape. I think the color scheme I went with was purple and gold, and I kind of went overboard. The chief stew shut me down and told me it was too extreme. Initially, I thought, *Well, I'm obviously not very good at setting tables,* but I wanted to prove myself.

A few years later, in my first role as chief stewardess, I was asked to put together an event in St. Tropez. I had an unlimited budget for a party of forty people. I picked a blue-and-white color

During my eight years in the yachting industry, I have crossed the Atlantic Ocean twice!

scheme and dove in. I ordered two incredible ice sculptures—they were so big we had to use a crane to get them on board—and hung a huge blue orchid curtain that stretched across the entire deck. I think I spent somewhere around forty thousand euros on the party, and the client was just blown away. It was freakin' awesome! It was a challenge, for sure—I had the deckhands wiping up all the water as the ice sculptures melted in the heat! But that was a defining moment for me. From then on, I became more and more keen to excel in the tablescaping and entertaining space.

ON BOARD AND ON TV

When I first joined *Below Deck*, I was very self-conscious about being in front of the camera. I'm an outgoing person, but it can be overwhelming when you have a camera in front of your face, and you know you are going to be broadcast everywhere. Anything you do wrong will be seen by hundreds of thousands of people, so I didn't really open myself up to the viewers during that first season (season 2). I'm a very unique character; I'm out there and I have a lot of quirks. Going back on the show for season 5 allowed me to return with a more confident mentality. I wanted to show the world who I was and to be true to myself. Whatever your opinion of me, like me or not, I had to be myself!

It was exciting that the show's producers focused so much on the tablescapes in season 5. Themes are a huge part of charters, and the guests are always requesting them. I wanted to show the world how we tablescape as stews. I wanted to bring that WOW factor into people's living rooms, because I didn't think tablescapes and entertaining always got enough credit on the show. I went out one day and bought a whole lot of décor. My goal was to always create that extra WOW factor—to go above and beyond in an attempt to get noticed. And boy, did I! I joke sometimes that some of my 'scapes could be considered the best two hundred euros I ever spent.

CREATIVITY UNLOCKED

I've dedicated this book to Chris, who inspired me in more ways than I could have ever imagined. He is an incredible man, and I was so privileged to work for him. I'd been the chief stew on his yacht for about a year, and when he decided to sell it, he asked me to come and manage the hospitality on his private island in the Bahamas. It was a life-changing opportunity. There, I headed up everything that had to do with hospitality and guest relations. I learned to provision—procuring items for a private island where our only mode of transport was by boat or seaplane.

I hosted dozens of fun parties there, and my boss absolutely loved a theme. He was the one who truly inspired my dream for theme. Chris provided me with a reasonable budget and a small team to work with that would allow my vision to flourish. Working with three carpenters, we created the most enchanting experiences. We'd use old wooden pallets and random pieces of bamboo to build teepees and shelters that I could drape material over and string fairy lights between, using pops of color and lanterns. Chris was also very big into candles and lighting. The more I worked with him, the more I realized how important it is to create an experience on a table that everyone can enjoy.

There was so much room for improvisation in my role there—that is where my creativity in that space was unlocked. When I left the island and rejoined the *Below Deck* crew, I was so confident in my skills and my style of entertaining and tablescaping.

WHY I LOVE TABLESCAPING

I could talk about tablescaping for days. There's no limit to what I love about it. I joke that it's a weird hobby to have, but it's the place where I go into a complete focus zone. Nothing can distract me from the task at hand. It's the only thing I've ever experienced in my thirty years of living that has kept me captivated. It's my calling.

There are no rules when it comes to tablescaping!

Sure, you can set the table with standard place settings and a vase of flowers in the middle, and no one is going to complain. But if your goal is a memorable get-together, a dazzling holiday dinner, or a party that will leave people talking, a detailed tablescape creates an adventure for the eye that your guests will love. People talk about "less is more," but I say, "more is more." As long as everything's placed correctly, and your color scheme is on point, it's always OK to go over the top. You don't need permission to have fun.

I have a very unique style. Although I incorporate flowers, you won't find me using standard, standalone floral arrangements. Instead, I focus on having different and unexpected elements. You can bring your own personal style to your tablescapes. I'm hoping this will be a guide that gives readers the framework to realize their own visions.

A tablescape should be an adventure. I love to create the story and the journey for the guests, giving them something to look at and talk about while they enjoy their meal. The food goes hand in hand with the tabletop design, so I will often collaborate with the chef to align the entire experience. Anyone can do this on their own scale. I may have a super-yacht budget for my tablescapes, but nothing I do needs to be expensive or too luxe. Even in my own home, I like to inspire that same sense of discovery through my tablescapes. With a few special objects, colors, and textures, a tablescape can take a person back in their memories to a different time or place. It should create a story, something memorable that will spark conversation and create nostalgia. It's a journey. You just never know what might be around the next corner.

The most fulfilling moments of creating the art on the table are seeing the reactions of the people who are dining—hearing what the décor might remind them of, and what they can relate to. I love to see how guests respond to the 'scapes I've designed. My wish is for readers of *The Art of Tablescaping* to experience the same sense of discovery.

COMMON MISCONCEPTIONS ABOUT TABLESCAPING

"EVERYTHING HAS TO BE FANCY."

Nope! Never be afraid to use things that might look cheap or tacky on their own. You can take strange or silly objects and place them with expensive elements or fresh flowers to elevate the whole design.

"BUYING THE SUPPLIES IS GOING TO BE EXPENSIVE."

On the boat, we don't always have a ton of storage or a massive décor budget to spend, so being able to repurpose objects or use everyday items is vital when I'm creating . . . and it can also be a lot of fun.

"I DON'T KNOW ALL THE DESIGN RULES."

There are absolutely no rules when it comes to tablescapes. Have fun with it. Be yourself! Show who you are through your tables and something magical will happen.

I FOUND THIS OLD piece of wood on the beach and repurposed it as a unique coaster/tray.

HOW TO GET STARTED

Building a tablescape is like constructing a house—you work from the base up. My theme and color scheme form an important part of my foundation. Next, I think about shapes, angles, and textures and how to work with them to enhance the table's concept. I move on to height and placement to create a journey for the eye, then look at adding pops of sparkle, light, and unexpected fun. Finally, I think beyond my table to tie the whole event together—drinks, food, party attire, and atmosphere.

In **SECTION 1** of this book, we'll walk through how to build your table by exploring all the elements you need to be thinking about to produce an unforgettable tablescape. Then, in **SECTION 2**, we'll look at some of my favorite themes to inspire your tablescaping adventures. Throughout the book, keep an eye out for lessons I've learned from my career as a stew, ideas to level up your table décor, suggestions for adding creative accents, and tips for transforming everyday objects into extraordinary design elements.

When I set a table, here's the basic formula that I use: color + texture + height = an adventure for the eye.

As you get started, remember: Have fun! Use what you have at home. Never be afraid to break any rules—because there *are* no rules. Pull out what you've got and give it a try. You can be as creative as your heart desires, and that's the beauty of it. Whatever inspires you is what is going to show through in your tablescape. Make your table something you enjoy, and I guarantee your guests will love it, too.

BUILD YOUR TABLE

THE ESSENTIAL ELEMENTS

Almost every table will have these important components—the exception being a cocktail party where guests will stand and mingle rather than sit.

CROCKERY
Porcelain or ceramic plates
Wooden boards
Slate plates

GLASSWARE
Colorful goblets
Crystal stemware
Stemless glasses
Acrylic tumblers

CUTLERY
Stainless steel
Silver, gold, or copper
Colorful acrylic
Chopsticks

NAPKINS
Paper
Cotton
Linen
Silk

OPTIONAL
Coasters
Chargers

When creating your tablescape, think about how you'll incorporate these essential items into the design. The glass you drink from and the plate you eat off can be—and usually are—design elements in their own right.

HEIGHT/PLACEMENT Use the various decorative elements of your 'scape to pull the eye along an interesting path, traveling up, down, and across the whole table.

FOUNDATION Your theme and color scheme, as well as the base layers that the rest of the décor is grounded on.

ATMOSPHERE How your food, drinks, music, and space tie in with the theme of your table.

CENTERPIECE A focal point for guests' attention, and a central piece or collection of décor that the rest of the design flows away from or toward.

SHAPES/ANGLES/TEXTURE Rough and smooth, round and sharp, the parts of your table that add the most contrast and visual interest.

BLING/SPARKLE The points of light, as well as the glittery and colorful extras that fill out your 'scape.

THE FOUNDATION

THEME, COLOR SCHEME, SPACE, AND TABLE BASE

Just as it does for a house, a strong foundation for your table will set you up for success. The foundation of a tablescape includes the guiding elements of your table's design—the theme and color scheme—but it also includes the space you have to work with and the pieces that form the 'scape's bottom layer: your tablecloth, runners, and placemats. When I'm working out my table's foundation, I think first about theme and color, then look at my table and the space on it and around it to plan the base layer of my 'scape.

Sometimes my theme and foundation have little bits that represent me hidden within them. Those are my favorite tables. For instance, I've created tables where I use a fishing net on the table as a runner. I grew up by the beach, and my career has been in yachting, so incorporating the sea is very personal to me. When you're laying your table's foundation, think about what's important to you and what glimpses of yourself you want your guests to see.

CHOOSING YOUR THEME

A theme can be very loose, but it can be helpful to think in general terms about the type of gathering you're planning: Is it outdoors (page 81), elegant (page 99), whimsical (page 117), or glam (page 147)? Is there a specific holiday you're celebrating (page 169)? Then narrow it down to specifics, such as a color, a place, or an idea. Whether you're gathering to celebrate a birthday, watch a favorite show, or throw a party just because, your theme will guide you and help you make decisions as you're building your table. Here are some ideas to jump-start your brainstorming:

WHAT'S THE OCCASION?

- Holiday
- Birthday
- Milestone
- Family gathering
- Just for the fun of it!

WHAT'S THE SEASON?

- Which colors do you associate with the season?
- Which kinds of fruits and plants are in season?
- Where do you live? Will the party be indoors or outdoors?

WHAT'S YOUR INSPIRATION?

- Special hobby
- Exciting era
- Favorite book, movie, or TV show
- Favorite color
- Favorite travel destination
- Someone's passion

WHICH ADJECTIVES WOULD SOMEONE USE TO DESCRIBE YOUR EVENT?

- Fun
- Luxe
- Over-the-top
- Laid-back
- Funky

Don't be afraid to go against the grain with unusual color schemes.

Still feeling stuck? See "[Fill in the Blank] Inspiration" on page 218 for a Mad Libs–inspired brainstorm.

INSPIRED BY AN AFTERNOON snorkeling in the Bahamas near Pablo Escobar's sunken plane, I re-created the scene in a glass bowl. The blue food coloring brought the Bahamian water to the table.

FUN TIP: Include Polaroids on the table to personalize the experience.

WORKING WITH COLOR

Be brave and mix unexpected colors. Don't be afraid to use color and metallics, either. I'm all about experimenting—putting things together helps you see what works and what doesn't. A lot of the time I pile things on the table, only to rip them off again, but you'll be surprised by the interesting combinations you'll discover by just playing around. Keep these ideas in mind as you get started:

CONTRASTING/COMPLEMENTARY COLORS

Life is all about balance. If I've got a room with cool colors, I might warm it up with wood and burnt-orange accents on the table.

DIFFERENT SHADES

I love to mix different shades of the same color—it will make your décor feel less flat. If everything is matchy-matchy, your eye will grow bored quickly.

METALLICS

There is absolutely nothing wrong with mixing silver and gold. You can even add a rose gold, copper, or bronze into the mix! Combining metals actually elevates the table quite a lot.

PATTERNS

Floral, tartan, dotted, striped—I love a good pattern. Be bold and try mixing different designs. They might clash, but they might also make for something fun and unexpected!

FOR A SPIN ON a fall tablescape, use unconventional colors for an otherwise traditional experience. This Thanksgiving 'scape uses blues and greens and elevates with silver, gold, and bronze.

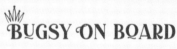

BUGSY ON BOARD

I'm always trying to surprise people with my tables, such as a fall seasonal tablescape that uses blues, greens, silvers, golds, or pinks—not the typical neutrals and oranges. On one yacht, we were celebrating Thanksgiving. Instead of the traditional colors and theme, I went with silver and green as my main colors and added lots of texture. The result was something shimmery and elegant.

WORKING WITH YOUR SPACE

Once you're starting to get a good sense of your theme and color scheme, take a close look at the space and the table. Here are some things to think about as you begin to visualize how your décor will take shape:

TABLE SHAPE AND SIZE

- **Is your table round or rectangular? Small or large?** Assess the space before buying or gathering materials; otherwise, you run the risk of the runner being too short or too long or placemats not fitting.
- **How tall is your décor?** Nothing on the table should block the guests' view of one another.
- **How many people will you be entertaining?** This will help you decide whether to go intimate or over the top in your décor.
- **Will guests be seated cozily around the table or have a lot of room to spread out?** You don't want your guests so far apart they have to raise their voices or so close they have no elbow room.
- **Are you creating a seating chart, or will guests be free to seat themselves?** For assigned seats, homemade place markers are a personal and helpful touch.

UNDERSTANDING THE SPACE

- **Are you inside or outside?** If you're outside, weather will play a role. Wind and rain can destroy even the best-planned tablescape.
- **How will guests enter?** What will they see first? A focal point will help set the stage for the event.
- **Where will they congregate?** Think about flow—if you've ever had your guests stuck in the kitchen all night, you know how important this is!

TABLE TIP

While you're setting your table, do some trial runs: sit down and pretend you're the guest to see if the setting works. Make sure guests can see each other's faces and that nothing is blocking them from one another or an amazing view. All of your décor should be arranged at a height that allows your guests to enjoy the setting, carry on conversations, and admire the table.

BUILDING YOUR TABLE'S BASE LAYER

Now it's time to start setting up your table. The first step is your base layer. If you've got a beautiful wooden or stone table, you may choose to forgo a base layer entirely to play up that amazing texture. Otherwise, think of adding one or several of these elements to lay the foundation for your design:

- Tablecloth
- Runner
- Placemats

8 ALTERNATIVES TO A TABLECLOTH

1. Layered placemats

2. Newspaper (stained with tea bags for a vintage look)

3. Nets

4. Burlap

5. Butcher paper—bonus if you include pens or pencils for sketching

6. Tulle

7. Overlapping doilies or lace

8. A long runner, or several shorter runners draped diagonally across the table

TABLESCAPING 101: FAMILY-STYLE MEALS

Most of the tablescapes in this book have décor at the table's center—not food. But a fun alternative is a big family-style meal where the food itself occupies center stage and is part of your tablescape. If you're doing that, look for serving platters and bowls with character, and surround them with objects that visually tie them together. Set the table with the platters first, so you can ensure there's enough space for them on the table. Think about layering platters so there's something lovely on the table when the guests arrive, then set the food platters on top when it's time to eat. The layers below should be a different color to add contrast. Make sure your meal has some showstopping elements in the food itself—and don't forget the serving utensils!

TYING IT ALL TOGETHER

Do you have a strong foundation? Here are some questions to ask yourself to see if you've got all your bases covered before you move on to decorating:

- How does my base layer complement my theme? (Organic? Luxurious? Festive? Outdoorsy? Casual?)

- Which colors have I already used in my foundation? Which colors am I going to play with in the rest of the décor?

- Do I have a plan for how to handle seating guests? Is there space for everyone?

- Will I be serving plated or family-style?

SHAPES, ANGLES & TEXTURE

CREATING VISUAL INTEREST THAT FITS YOUR THEME

Are you ready to start building up from your foundation? Shapes, angles, and texture are the language you use to begin to tell your table's story. They enhance one another and allow you to evoke specific moods and eras. The shapes and angles you use determine the flow of your table. The lines in these forms will direct your eye around the table, from the edges to the centerpiece and back again. The texture creates the overall feel of your table.

You want your décor to be fun and fresh—the talk of the table. Mixing and matching elements of shape, angle, and texture allows you to create natural talking points that ripple across the surface of your tablescape.

WORKING WITH DIFFERENT SHAPES AND ANGLES

Just like when you're working with color, using a variety of shapes and angles on your table is best. Try pairing items that are round and oblong with those that are rectangular and sharp for a balanced effect.

ROUND AND OBLONG

- Round tablecloths and placemats
- Circular or spherical vases
- Flowers with large blossoms
- Most citrus fruits
- Glass pebbles
- Petals
- Beads or marbles
- Round leaves

ANGULAR AND SHARP

- Table runners
- Rectangular placemats
- Books
- Square and rectangular vases
- Grasses
- Palm fronds
- Pyramids, crystals, or other angular objects
- Artichokes, pineapples, and pine cones

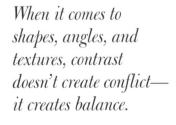

When it comes to shapes, angles, and textures, contrast doesn't create conflict— it creates balance.

EVERYDAY EXTRAORDINARY

In your house right now you probably have loads of items that already mix and match shapes and angles. Just find décor in your kitchen or vegetable/fruit basket! I use vegetables and fruits all the time in my tablescapes. I usually scatter them around the table, but other times they form the basis of an amazing centerpiece. Some of my favorites are artichokes, lemons, pomegranates, and pineapples, but there are so many to choose from. You can leave them whole or slice them in half for extra color and texture. You can even dehydrate citrus wheels for an interesting alternative. Walk through the grocery store and get inspired.

WORKING WITH DIFFERENT TEXTURES

I'm usually of the opinion that the more textures you have on your table, the better. They add visual interest to your spread. If you've got a lot of soft, flowy material on your table, add in some spiky or rough elements to set it off—or vice versa. Try any of the following textures layered around your table as needed:

FABRICS

- Burlap—rough and organic
- Linen—natural but refined
- Satin—smooth and shiny
- Tulle—frothy and fancy
- Lace—intricate and delicate

NATURAL ELEMENTS

- Twisty branches
- Round or jagged river rocks or sea glass
- Dried flowers
- Scattered petals
- Leaves and grasses
- Fruits, vegetables, nuts, and seeds
- Dried citrus fruits
- Seashells
- Coffee beans

FUN EXTRAS

- Coiled rope
- Draped fishing nets
- Glitter or confetti of different shapes and sizes
- Strands of beads, pearls, glass, etc.
- Different colors of cellophane
- Old wine corks

TABLE TIP

Fresh flowers are always a key element in any table design. You've got the objects and all these cool items and artifacts, but when you add the fresh flowers, it brings it all to life.

THIS HAVANA-NIGHTS evening incorporated lots of fun extras to evoke a Cuban celebration. I found a vintage cigar tin in a thrift shop and paired it with dehydrated citrus, fresh pomegranates, and some gorgeous florals!

NAPKINS FOR ALL OCCASIONS

Whatever the event, you're going to need napkins.
What kind you use depends on your theme and
the general feeling of your event.

- **COCKTAIL NAPKINS**—for an event without
  place settings, where guests are circling the
  table and eating finger foods
- **PAPER NAPKINS**—very informal and casual
- **COTTON NAPKINS**—the practical choice
- **LINEN NAPKINS**—classy and classic
- **SILK NAPKINS**—luxe and fancy

EVERYDAY EXTRAORDINARY

Create your own napkin rings with empty toilet-paper tubes—just cut them in half and wrap them with twine, burlap, cloth, or paper.

PUT A RING ON IT

For tablescapes with a lot of detail, I like to keep the napkin fold simple, which usually means napkin rings. You can find so many different beautiful napkin rings out there. Wood, metal, and glass are all classic options. A fun way to use napkin rings is to make little bows with your napkins. Fold a square napkin into an upside-down triangle. Turn the triangle sideways by rotating 90 degrees. Starting at the top, thread the triangle through the napkin ring until the ring is in the middle, and place it on the plate. Fold the corners to make a bow.

ESSENTIAL NAPKIN FOLDS

Nothing adds texture, shape, and finesse to your table like a thoughtfully folded napkin. For all of these folds, start with an ironed square dinner napkin. You can lightly spray the napkin with starch to ensure the napkin holds the fold. Think hair spray!

HEART FOLD

1. Fold in half to form a rectangle, then in half again lengthwise to make a thinner rectangle with the open end facing up.

2. From the middle of the napkin, bring the right side up so that it's perpendicular to the original rectangle. Do the same on the left side. You should now have a V at the bottom, with the two sides next to each other along the middle and flat at the top.

3. Fold the top interior portion of each side under so that the center meets in a V shape.

4. Now fold the tops down to make an angular heart shape.

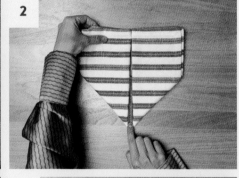

TABLE TIP

In a pinch, I've literally just tied napkins into a knot. It looks neat and chic on the table, and is something different. Everyone is used to napkin rings or special kinds of folds, but this is so simple and really effective.

CASCADING TRIANGLE FOLD

1. Fold in half to form a rectangle, then half again to form a square. Position the napkin like a diamond with the open end facing up.

2. Take the very top layer of the napkin and fold it down to form a triangle that stops about one inch from the bottom of your diamond.

3. Fold the next layer down so that it rests about half an inch from the previous fold. Do the same with the next two layers.

4. Flip the napkin over so that the point is facing up, then fold in the two sides to overlap.

5. Flip it over again for the final presentation.

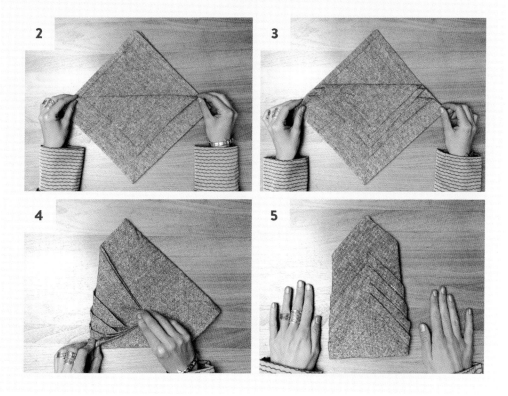

ROSE FOLD

1. Fold in half to form a triangle.

2. With the folded edge facing you, (a) roll up about two-thirds of the way to the tip of the triangle, then (b) roll up entirely from one side, (c) tucking the remaining tail into the surrounding folds to secure.

3. (a) Pull apart the triangular tip, then turn the napkin over to reveal your rose and two leaves (b).

2a

2b

2b

2c

3a

3b

LOTUS FOLD

1. Fold all four corners in, then fold all four corners in again.

2. Flip the whole thing over, then fold all four corners in once more.

3. (a) Pull out the edges under each corner to secure the petals and form your leaves, and (b) you have your little lotus flower.

IT'S ALL ABOUT THE GLASS

Glass naturally adds sparkle and shine, smooth surfaces, and interesting angles. Use glass in various forms around your table to enhance and set off the shapes, angles, and textures already in play. Think beyond beverages! You can also incorporate glass into serving dishes, centerpieces, and other decorative elements.

CONSIDER THE FOLLOWING TYPES OF
GLASSWARE TO WORK WITH YOUR THEME:

- Crystal-cut glass for glittery sophistication
- Glass in vibrant colors to enhance or complement your color scheme
- Mason jars for a rustic, rural feel
- Milk glass or opaque glass for a vintage look
- Interesting bottles to add texture and height
- Glass tea light candle holders or vases

EVERYDAY EXTRAORDINARY

Fill a variety of glass jars and vases with water, then dye with food coloring to match or complement your color scheme. They can become the bases for floating candles and flowers or call attention to an object of interest within.

IN THIS 'SCAPE, I mixed height and various shades of the same color to create an incredible experience for the eye. These water/wine glasses aren't your traditionally shaped goblets, but who doesn't like to spice things up?!

TABLESCAPING 101: CHARGER PLATES

What is a "charger plate" and when should you use one? A charger plate holds a place on your table for the eventual plates that will go there. It should be decorative and make a statement. When it's time to serve, you'll put the crockery on top of the charger plates. Charger plates are great for adding shape and texture to your table from the get-go, and they create an elegant mood.

TYING IT ALL TOGETHER

Contrast is key to creating interesting energy.
Try to incorporate contrasting shapes, angles,
and textures using all the elements of your table.
Here are some ideas to get you started:

- Try smooth and shiny napkins against a rough-textured table base.

- Pair glitzy, round metallic charger plates with crisply folded rectangular white napkins.

- Defy expectations with round placemats and square plates (or vice versa).

- Mix metal and glass with organic items, such as plants and flowers plucked right from your garden.

THE
CENTERPIECE

CHOOSING & CREATING
THE STAR OF THE SHOW

Your centerpiece is your crowning jewel. It's the focal point for the eye, the thing that pulls the theme and table design together. Your centerpiece illuminates your table's story. It's your main course. The rest of the table décor flows toward and away from it.

So how do you choose your centerpiece? Sometimes the centerpiece chooses you, and suddenly you're creating a theme and designing a table around a stunning piece of vintage glassware or gorgeous arrangement of flowers—or even a broken-down boat propeller that you rescued from the trash. Or, if you already have your theme and your color scheme in mind, it's up to you to find or create a centerpiece that completes your vision.

WHAT MAKES A GOOD CENTERPIECE?

Need some inspiration for your centerpiece? Here are some ideas to get you started. You don't need to stick to any one category. Follow your intuition and mix and match as you please.

STATEMENT OBJECTS
- Figurines
- Decorative glass, wood, or metal pieces
- Vintage items

COLLECTIONS
- Objects that tell a story when grouped together
- Several vases of different heights

SCULPTURAL FLORAL ARRANGEMENTS
- Branches, leaves, or moss to add texture
- Feathers, cloth, or non-organic items to add visual interest

CENTRAL POINTS OF LIGHT
- Vases filled with fairy lights
- Lighted text or signs
- Large arrangement of votive candles

POTTED PLANTS WITH TEXTURE
- Succulents
- Cacti
- Ferns

EVERYDAY OBJECTS REIMAGINED
- Empty champagne bottles topped with dripping candles
- Swing-top bottles filled with jewel-toned glass

HANGING ELEMENTS
- Cloth
- Macramé
- Trailing vines
- . . . and many more

Remember, a centerpiece doesn't have to be a huge vase of flowers. Try looking around your house or your garden. Keep an eye out at thrift stores. Look for items with interesting shapes or textures, and start playing!

FINDING BALANCE AT YOUR TABLE

The design elements on your table should speak in harmony. The centerpiece might be the loudest, but the other elements on the table want to have their voices heard, too.

- Make the centerpiece part of a pattern in the table design, with different elements repeating here and there along the whole tablescape.
- Try organized chaos on your table—a heap of fun and colorful items that are actually carefully positioned to lead toward a few central objects.
- Lift your centerpiece above the other elements of the table, like the peak of a mountain, and have the rest of the table décor cascade down toward the edges.

BUGSY ON BOARD

Even something that looks like junk might be the perfect object to throw onto the center of a table and build a design around. When I found an old, bent propeller about to be thrown out, I knew it was a diamond in the rough. We were in the Bahamas with a group of guests who went to visit Pablo Escobar's crashed plane, which is a propeller plane. So the old propeller became the central element of my Pablo Escobar–themed tablescape. Propellers have such a great combination of sharp and soft angles—plus it was the perfect talking point. The crew was like, "What are you doing? You can't put that on the table." But I did, and it was a huge hit with the guests.

5 WAYS TO USE A VASE AS A CENTERPIECE

1. Use several vases of different heights to create tiers of floral arrangements.

2. Fill them with colored glass, beads, marbles, or even candy.

3. Make a vase into a terrarium.

4. Fill several vases with river rocks or sand and use them as large candleholders.

5. Turn one upside down and fill it with tulle, long-lasting flowers, or fairy lights.

THE CENTERPIECE dominates the table, but it should work in concert with all the other elements of the design.

TABLESCAPING 101: CREATING ECHOES

An echo is a softer version of a sound you've already heard. Make visual echoes of your centerpiece around the table to give the whole design a unified, cohesive feel.

- If you have a large central flower arrangement, place smaller groupings of similar flowers around your table.

- Choose one color from your centerpiece, then use glassware or similar-toned pebbles or glitter in that color around the table.

- Show the textures of your centerpiece in the rest of your table—think scraps of frothy tulle, smooth and shiny leaves, or crinkled cellophane.

- Place sharp or soft angled elements around the table to accentuate a spiky or smooth centerpiece.

"BE HAPPY AND BRIGHT!" This theme resonates with my personality. In looking for a table that would bring cheer to my guests, I chose my favorite bright colors and threw them all together!

TYING IT ALL TOGETHER

You want to make sure your centerpiece, theme, and color palette live harmoniously in your eyes. The essential elements of your table help everything work together.

TRY A FEW OF THESE SIMPLE IDEAS:

- Match the napkin color to something in your centerpiece.
- Place a metallic element in your centerpiece to tie in with the shine of your cutlery or charger plates (if using).
- Use white porcelain plates with central vases of white flowers.

HEIGHT & PLACEMENT

CREATING A JOURNEY FOR THE EYE

Your tablescape works best when it's an adventure for the eye. All the little details should fall at different places and heights across the table. When you've kept height and placement in mind while designing, your tablescape becomes like a game of I spy, with guests noticing special touches depending on where they're seated at the table, which in turn sparks conversations.

As you work with height and placement at your table, think about creating a path for the eye to follow. If your theme is Gatsby (see page 164), you might build a story that travels from tall alcohol bottles draped with pearls down to a glitter-strewn table set with old-fashioned champagne glasses—and maybe even a fancy shoe that your guests can imagine was kicked off by a raucous flapper. If your theme is tropical, your eye might travel from tall, breezy palm fronds down to tropical fruits and citrus that evoke warmth and sunshine (see page 90).

HEIGHT

Height isn't just about what's up at the top level of your tablescape—it's also what's down toward the bottom. When you think about height, you're thinking about all the levels of your design and how they work together. Here are some tips to keep in mind:

- You can't go high without going low! Don't forget to offset the tall points on your table with interesting bits lower down.
- Remember that while the centerpiece is often the highest point on the table, it doesn't have to be! Feel free to play around with different high points.
- If you are wondering how high you can go, sit at each location at the table and make sure that your guests' sight lines are going to be accessible.

BUGSY ON BOARD

Once on a yacht I created this insane masterpiece. It took me so much time—gathering all the flowers, little bits and pieces—and when I finished, I stood back from the table and admired it. I was so excited for my guests to see it. But the minute they sat down, they couldn't see each other. So all the beauty I'd created ended up getting taken off the table. Now it's my number-one rule: make sure you are able to see the people sitting across from you.

EVERYDAY EXTRAORDINARY

Create height variety by using regular items in unexpected ways. Fill a brandy or wine glass with tulle, turn it upside down, and top with a candle. Hang items from a central light fixture. Use cake stands to lift your décor off the table.

PLACEMENT

Arranging a tablescape is a lot like arranging a vase of flowers. You put something in, step back to look at it, then maybe adjust it slightly or move it somewhere else. There's a lot of placing and replacing going on, especially once you get started. It's all about finding balance around the table. Here are some ideas to keep in mind as you work:

- Scatter items on the table to get started, then gently adjust their spacing so there are no gaping holes or clusters.
- Always move around the table as you place items so you can see them from all angles.
- Set items with similar shapes at different angles on the table.
- Explore the edges of your table—how far can you pull your tablescape outward?
- If you really want an item to stand out, make sure it has some space. I often find a couple of items that really mean something to me and put them in a central location. The other elements of the table point toward those items.

THE CHAMPAGNE for this event came in these bronze cages, which I repurposed as candleholders. They help anchor the other metallic elements on the table while also adding warmth.

TABLE TIP

Remember: your centerpiece and the surrounding décor might look good from one angle, but if you completely forget about the people sitting across from it, the design could be one-sided. For example, a sculpture might look fabulous to the person facing it, but the guests on the other side of the table have to look at its backside all night! You want to achieve a well-rounded look at the whole table as you go.

TABLESCAPING 101: TALKING POINTS

Talking points are those fun little pieces that raise eyebrows, evoke nostalgia, and get people talking. Don't be afraid to use items that seem a little funky or weird—a beaded camel, a ceramic elephant, or dollar-store souvenirs. Fun and unique items like that bring the whole table to life. I love going to thrift shops to search for little knickknacks to inspire future tables. Every time I step into a thrift shop, it's like I'm going into a dreamland. There are so many whimsical things you can pick off the shelves, and they have such a story to them, which I love to bring to the table.

TYING IT ALL TOGETHER

Now it's all about spacing. After your table is nearly set, take a few laps around it to look at how everything is spaced in your design. Here are some questions I ask myself as I go:

- Did I go overboard? Is my décor overshadowing itself? As much as I love to always go for something extra, sometimes I have to take a few things off the table at the last minute to avoid overwhelming the theme I'm going for. You don't want your exuberant designs to come off as cluttered.

- Does everyone have an interesting angle? Remember to take a moment to sit in each guest's seat. Think about how they will interact with the table, and whether you need to move anything closer to or farther away from certain seats.

- Do my various heights work with my centerpiece? Is everything moving toward that point? Do the centerpiece and the other pieces complement each other?

BLING & SPARKLE

THAT LITTLE SOMETHING EXTRA

This might just be the best part of tablescaping: when your table is just about done, it's time to accessorize. Just like putting on jewelry, your favorite hair clips, or that perfect lipstick before you go out, adding the exciting extras really gets you in the mood for a party. My favorite accessories to take your table over the top? Lights and glitter, of course, as well as pops of color. Heirlooms, antiques, and other treasures also add a special touch.

ALL THAT GLITTERS AND SHINES

Transforming your tablescape from a daytime event to a nighttime one can be as simple as adding some light. Here are ways to incorporate lights into your tablescape:

- Real candles
- Battery-operated candles
- Floating candles
- Fairy lights
- Glass lanterns
- Paper lanterns
- Tea lights in holders
- Colorful light-up balls
- Tiki torches

Never underestimate the power of lighting. Think about the fluorescent overheads in a dentist's office; now picture the warm glow of a candelabra. Lighting in your space is just as important as the lighting on your table. Make sure you have enough light to see your meal, but not so much that you lose the magic.

BUGSY ON BOARD

I like to use a lot of battery-operated candles
and tea lights because I'm used to tablescaping
on yachts and we are not always allowed to use
fire on the boat. But flameless candles are also
great for outdoors, when wind can snuff out
your candles, or when integrating candles into
a 'scape with lots of flammable materials (like
tulle or other fabrics). It's also nice to not spend
your night swapping out tea lights!

IT'S ALL ABOUT sparkles. Here I've included
three different spheres that are made of glitter
and crystals and then scattered a few glass
rhinestones in between.

THE LITTLE THINGS GO A LONG WAY

Get creative with the little bits and pieces that liven up your table. Here are some ideas to get you started:

- Go down to your local florist and pick out bright and colorful flowers to sprinkle around. Many florists also sell buckets of flower petals. These add an instant feeling of luxury.
- For a playful circus feel, pop some popcorn in your microwave and scatter it on the table.
- Add instant fun with bright, shiny sweets and lollipops.
- Incorporate glass pebbles, my all-time favorite way to add some extra sparkle.
- Sprinkle confetti around your table to say "Party!" right away.
- Use wooden or rattan balls to tie into larger themes of shape and texture that you're working with.
- Keep an eye out at thrift stores or dollar stores for colorful smaller objects that can double as guest favors to be snatched off the table. (Check out the mini maracas in my Mexican fiesta 'scape on page 130.)
- Need some emergency glitter and shine? Wrap objects in or create shapes with kitchen aluminum foil to add a touch of silver sparkle.

I like to use protea flowers in my tablescapes when I can. The protea is the national flower of South Africa, where I'm from. It's wonderful to incorporate some of your roots into your table as a tribute to who you are. If you have an antique lying around, a family heirloom, or a favorite flower, that simple touch can be a fantastic talking point. Always try to incorporate an item that will spark conversation.

EVERYDAY EXTRAORDINARY

Searching for something to take your tablescape up a notch? Your home is probably already full of interesting little objects to enhance your décor. Scatter puzzle pieces and old wine corks alongside maps and gold trinkets to make your guests feel that they're in for a night of adventure and excitement.

ATMOSPHERE

BEYOND YOUR TABLESCAPE

T he table is set—now you're ready to set the mood. My three favorite ways to pull together the final pieces for an event are planning the music, choosing a signature drink, and pulling out all the stops with my own outfit.

SIGNATURE DRINK

If my table is sparkly, I might go with something bubbly for my signature cocktail. If I'm going vintage, I might stick with a classic martini or Manhattan. Something with rum, tequila, or mezcal—or a selection of beautiful fruit juices—complements a tropical theme. If I'm going for loose and relaxed, I might pair some really excellent beer or bottles of Coca-Cola with my table. Rosé is one of my favorite wines to incorporate. The color adds a beautiful blush to your table, even if the central color scheme isn't pink.

MUSIC

Music is such a natural way to enhance your table. If your table evokes a certain era, play music from that time. If your theme is a country, spend some time searching for selections you like by musicians from that place. And if all else fails, a playlist of your all-time favorites makes a great conversation starter.

OUTFIT

The ultimate: dress like your tablescape. I especially love to dress like my most colorful tables—the bigger and brighter, the better. Sequins, fun fabrics, pops of color, vibrant makeup, and statement jewelry are all ways you can dress to complement your table.

TABLE TIP

Grab a couple of rolls of ticket coupons, which you can find at any party store. They add a fun carnival or circus vibe to your 'scape, but you can also use these tickets to create a game while you're sitting at the table. Have a raffle, write and pass notes . . . You can make it kid-friendly or adult-friendly, depending on your guests.

I try to think about my guests when I'm preparing my atmosphere. If not everyone drinks alcohol, I make sure to have a special signature mocktail ready to go. If I know someone loves a specific song, I sneak it onto the playlist.

INSPIRATION

OUTDOORS

From a low-key picnic to an explosion of elegant pink, your outdoor dining can be as unique as you are. But while all of these themes work well in a yard or on a back deck in a warm climate or during the summer, remember that you can always take that outdoor inspiration inside during the colder months. Light, airy décor is always welcome. Plants, flowers, grasses, and fruit can transform your dining room into a much-needed oasis.

TAME >>> WILD!

NEUTRAL >>> COLORFUL

EASY >>> DIFFICULT

SIGNATURE DRINK
Sauvignon blanc

COLOR SCHEME
Green, gold, and yellow

STATEMENT DÉCOR
*Picnic baskets,
grasses, and flowers*

PLAYLIST
*"Here Comes the Sun"
by the Beatles, "Sun is
Shining" by Bob Marley,
"Banana Pancakes" by
Jack Johnson*

PICNIC IN THE GRASS

EVOKE THE FEELING of a picnic in the grass with the essential comforts of home. Bunches of grasses and flowers make a sophisticated centerpiece feel relaxed and approachable.

CREATIVE ACCENTS

Vintage picnic baskets are a welcome addition to a lot of tablescapes, and they're absolutely perfect here. They're decorative but also very useful—I like to tuck an extra bottle of chilled white wine into a basket with a bouquet of simple flowers.

Try mixing sizes, colors, and textures of glassware.

A BEAUTIFUL, NATURAL WOOD surface needs very little in the way of a base layer. A thin runner and round placemats allow the grain of the wood to be the star of the show.

EVERYDAY EXTRAORDINARY

I love to use grasses in my tablescapes, especially if they've got a bit of fluff at the top and long, inviting stems. It adds a very modern look, but at the same time it's cost-effective and natural. You don't have to go to a florist to get a selection of interesting grasses to add texture to your tablescape. Just pick grasses when you're out for a walk and dry them! The same thing goes for leaves, shells, branches . . . Nature is filled with texture for your table.

A PILE OF CUSHIONS on the ground invites lounging and relaxing. Don't be afraid to forgo the chairs, push the couch or outdoor seating aside, and set your low-lying coffee table as a dining space.

How gorgeous is this napkin
flower? I've folded two napkins
with the lotus fold (see page 47),
then set one atop the other and
placed a little flower in the middle.

TAME ››› WILD!

NEUTRAL ››› COLORFUL

EASY ››› DIFFICULT

SIGNATURE DRINK
Sweet tea

COLOR SCHEME
Browns, metallics, purple, and orange

STATEMENT DÉCOR
Protea flowers, vintage vases, and woven mats

PLAYLIST
"She Moves in Her Own Way" by the Kooks, "Dancing in the Moonlight" by Jubël (featuring NEIMY), "Broken" by Lovelytheband

RUSTIC BEACH CHIC

THIS TABLE IS a lot like me. I'm a beachy girl, and I love the outdoors, but I also love the glitz and glamor and the high-end lifestyle. I wanted this table to be homey and inviting but also super chic and exciting.

TABLE TIP

Add warm gold charger plates, metallic vases, and grass placemats interwoven with silver to balance a natural and simple style with the luxurious and chic.

I LIKE AN OUTFIT that doesn't totally match my tablescape but enhances it. I love the way my gold hoops and straw hat highlight the table's contrast of natural and elegant.

TABLE TIP

Layering the base elements of your table creates an irresistible texture. Here I've used woven pieces with different sizes and structures. The stripes in the runner echo those in the grass placemats. On top of the runner, I've added a woven leaf and draped a vintage fishing net. The rattan balls are a sophisticated extension of the textures in these bottom layers.

Protea flowers are very durable and long-lasting, so you can reuse them a couple of times if you keep them in water. They look super gorgeous even if you dry them out.

I HAVE A COLLECTION of antique vases of different sizes and shapes. They allow you to create a lot of height, but I try to arrange them in a way so people can still see one another.

TROPICAL GETAWAY

TAME ››› WILD!

NEUTRAL ››› COLORFUL

EASY ››› DIFFICULT

SIGNATURE DRINK
Mai Tais

COLOR SCHEME
*Pink, green, and metallics
(gold and copper)*

STATEMENT DÉCOR
*Tropical fruit, palm
fronds, and tiki tumbler*

PLAYLIST
*"Are You with Me" by
Lost Frequencies, "Down
South" by Jeremy Loops,
"Paradise" by Meduza*

A TROPICAL PARTY is pure fun. You could sit at this table in a bathing suit, or you could wear your most colorful cocktail dress.

EVERYDAY EXTRAORDINARY

I love creating tables with items from nature—or the grocery store. We've got fresh fruits, fresh flowers, and bright colors. Some of the fruits are whole, and some have been cut in half to give that great color and texture. We found some palm fronds around the property that we repurposed into the tablescape. The coconuts required some creative thinking. I left some whole and cracked others in half. I didn't have a machete or a hammer around, so I actually used a brick to smash them apart. You've gotta do what you've gotta do. Improvisation is key when it comes to tablescapes, because not everything is going to go the way you planned.

It's a very natural table, but I've also included some elements such as a gold star and vases to give a contrasting glamor to the natural elements.

A LITTLE COLORED TUFT of grass in a vintage tiki tumbler makes for an instant talking point at the table's center.

TABLE TIP

For this table, I've gone with a mix of placemats—woven mats, circular gold stunners, and even large glossy leaves. The result is something loose and eclectic. For the beverages, I also tried to mix things up. The green glass goblets and the hammered copper Moscow Mule mugs match the colors of the table but increase the sophistication level of the whole affair.

If I'm going for a low-key vibe, I love to incorporate funky décor, like this beachy little sign. It made me laugh, so of course I just had to include it.

SIGNATURE DRINK
Sparkling rosé

COLOR SCHEME
Pink!

STATEMENT DÉCOR
*Gold lanterns
and metallic rope*

PLAYLIST
*"Pink + White" by
Frank Ocean, "Pink
Cashmere" by Prince,
"Baby" by Ariel Pink*

♛ PINK LADY

THIS THEME IS so versatile. You can use it for a hens' party (Americans call it a bachelorette party, right?), a girls' brunch, or really anything that you feel fits. Pretty in pink always works.

TABLE TIP

I've enhanced this table with beautiful pink metallic petrified roses, which you can pick up at most high-end florists. These flowers are a little bit on the pricy side, but at the end of the day it works out better because you can use them in so many different tablescapes, as well as around your house in your home décor.

A long white-and-gold rope winds throughout the center of the table, pulling all the elements together.

DO I REALLY need to say it? This table was *made* for rosé.

CREATIVE ACCENTS

I've reimagined how to use vintage lanterns here, turning them into vases for dyed grasses, petrified roses, and sparkly balls. They suggest light and flame but are soft and feminine at the same time. The dried grasses contrast nicely with the fresh roses on the napkins. Fresh roses are always a welcome touch.

*I love the angles on this tablecloth—
the design is modern and classic at
the same time—so I complemented
it with striped pink napkins, folded
so that the lines are going off at
interesting angles.*

ELEGANT

I obviously love to call myself the Queen of Theme, but that doesn't mean my table concepts are always obvious or over-the-top. A theme for me might be as simple as red and blue, or artichokes and lemons, and the result is a design that's eye-catching and spectacular. I've found that some of the most refined themes rely on simplicity—I focus on a color, a texture, an object, or a type of lighting for pure elegance.

SIGNATURE DRINK
Lemon Drop

COLOR SCHEME
Yellow, green, and gold

STATEMENT DÉCOR
*Artichokes and
vintage glassware*

PLAYLIST
*"Lemon Tree"
by the Ditty Bops,
"Lemon Firebrigade"
by Haircut 100*

ARTICHOKES & LEMONS

THIS THEME IS all about color, texture, and contrast. Smooth lemons and spiky artichokes are the bright points of focus, with the rest of the table playing off their traits in subtle ways.

CREATIVE ACCENTS

When your table's theme is simple and elegant, it's fun to find a way to enhance it with the beverages and atmosphere. For this table, I might fill two glass jugs with water—one with slices of lemon, another with slices of cucumber. It almost invites guests to pick a side: Are you team green or are you team yellow?

Overlapping placemats make one of my favorite base layers. They allow you to play with tone and texture in really interesting ways.

A STUNNER OF a gold antique vase and a collection of interesting bottles pull the design upward. I've filled them with angular golden-hued grasses and round yellow and green flowers, plus the globe of an artichoke.

Metallic tulle softens and unites the whole tablescape with its airy iridescence. The napkins have an unfinished, organic edge that echoes the softness of the tulle.

TABLE TIP

If contrast is important to your theme, find a way to use it in every part of the table. Here, I've used two runners—one that's smooth yellow and another that's roughly woven grass—to echo the characteristics of the lemons and artichokes. Smooth gold chargers sit on loosely woven gold placemats. I even have drinking glasses that are both yellow and smooth, and green and textured.

SIGNATURE DRINK
Sancerre

COLOR SCHEME
Blue, yellow, and gold

STATEMENT DÉCOR
A toy sailboat, rattan balls, and rope

PLAYLIST
"Jubel" by Klingande, "Crazy" by Lost Frequencies, "Intro" by the xx, "Cruising Through" by GoldFish

ABOVE THE WAVES

SET SAIL with a tablescape that works just as well for a morning brunch as it does for a dinner party. Here, a classic color scheme emerges from the perfect centerpiece object.

BUGSY ON BOARD

You get pretty good at a nautical theme when you've spent a few years creating tablescapes on yachts. I learned early on how to evoke the feeling of underwater reefs—small twisted sticks and dyed feathers or grasses in a vase become coral. Meanwhile, rattan balls have a very maritime feel to them, recalling floats and buoys. Of course you have to include rope or netting, and my favorite glass pebbles look like sea glass. A beautiful centerpiece object— like this sailboat—brings it all together.

This table takes me right back to working on a yacht in St. Tropez. Looking at it, I can see the wooden boats and electric blues of the harbor.

IF YOU DON'T HAVE an adorable toy sailboat of your own on hand, fold some newspaper boats for the middle of the table instead. They have a very nostalgic feel to them, and the text adds a cool pattern.

TABLE TIP

The centerpiece is very much in the middle of the table here. It's an intimate design. Rather than drawing the eye all around the table, it pulls the guests' eyes toward the center—and each other. The statement napkins bring design elements to the edges of the table without overwhelming the centerpiece.

Never underestimate the power of a simple napkin in a ring, fanned out into a circle. The wave-like folds go perfectly with my nautical theme.

TAME ››› WILD!

NEUTRAL ››› COLORFUL

EASY ››› DIFFICULT

SIGNATURE DRINK
Gin Fizz

COLOR SCHEME
Blue and gold

STATEMENT DÉCOR
*Ceramic puffer fish
and spiky ball*

PLAYLIST
*"The Island" by Skipinnish,
"Waves" (Robin Schulz
remix) by Mr. Probz,
"One Million Views" by
GoldFish, "Let Me Tell You
About My Boat" by Mark
Mothersbaugh*

BELOW THE WAVES

I CAN'T THINK OF anything more gorgeous than a coral reef. But rather than going with an over-the-top, colorful undersea adventure, I've chosen to keep the focus on a few specific textures found in that environment. The result is understated glamor.

TABLE TIP

Don't be afraid to layer on top of patterns. This tablecloth seems like it has a lot going on with its coral motif, but I layered a striped runner on top of it anyway. Instead of competing with the tablecloth, it actually allowed me to highlight some of the coral designs without overpowering my beautiful centerpiece objects.

YOU COULD EASILY make this tablescape evening-ready by stringing fairy lights around with the rope or placing a few low candles within the centerpiece arrangement.

CREATIVE ACCENTS

This centerpiece is all about the statement objects. They are so unique and fun to look at that they require very little embellishment, just the right arrangement to achieve balance.

This black-and-gold spiky ball instantly becomes a sea urchin in this tablescape. A textured flower tucked into a small gold candleholder looks just like an anemone.

RED AND BLUE

SIGNATURE DRINK
A peppery red wine

COLOR SCHEME
Red and blue

STATEMENT DÉCOR
*Simple flower arrangements
and stacks of balls*

PLAYLIST
*"Sweet Caroline" by
Neil Diamond, "This Is
How It Goes" by GoldFish,
"Brown Eyed Girl" by
Van Morrison, "We Didn't
Start the Fire" by Billy Joel*

**TWO GORGEOUS
COLORS,** cool and warm,
work together to create simple
elegance. A successful theme
doesn't have to be any more
complicated than this.

CREATIVE ACCENTS

Of course a good bottle of
red would go beautifully with
this tablescape, but when
your theme is simple, it's
fun to get creative with your
beverage pairings. Try floating
pomegranate seeds in a flute of
Prosecco to highlight the subtle
gold elements of the table, or
whip up a batch of sangria filled
with gorgeous red fruits.

A SINGLE PERFECT FLOWER nestled in an elegant dish makes a statement all on its own. No embellishment needed.

Color is king on this table, but it's the interacting textures of all the red and blue elements that keep the design from feeling flat—plus the occasional sparkle from the tablecloth and the glass goblets.

TABLE TIP

A vase of dried flowers is just as elegant as a vase of fresh blooms. Better yet, you can fill the vase itself with something other than water. In this tablescape, I've placed glass pebbles in the base of one vase but left the textural stems of the flowers visible. A round white incense holder, which resembles a sea urchin, becomes the base for a tiny but mighty arrangement of red and gold.

FUN & WHIMSICAL

Bright colors, big themes, over-the-top décor—that's how I have fun. My tablescapes can be delicate and subdued, but more often than not I go super big, super vibrant. It might be surprising, but I've found that tables with a lot going on are often the ones that put guests most at ease. The more there is to look at, the more immersed in the table you become, and conversation flows courtesy of one-of-a-kind centerpieces and dramatic, quirky place settings. So get silly, have fun, and lean into the whimsy around your table!

CARNIVAL

TAME ››› WILD!

NEUTRAL ››› COLORFUL

EASY ››› DIFFICULT

SIGNATURE DRINK
Anything bubbly!

COLOR SCHEME
The whole rainbow

STATEMENT DÉCOR
Vibrant masks and glittery confetti

PLAYLIST
"Don't Stop the Music" by Rihanna, "Wonderful" by Burna Boy, "Sun Is Shining" by Bob Marley & the Wailers

WHEN IT COMES TO major celebrations, more is more. We're talking carnival here! It's all about being over-the-top: lots of fun, lots of bright colors, and lots of different textures.

TABLE TIP

I love to tuck glittery points of light among the sparkles of the table. These LED tea lights are great—no fire hazards here—but candles in small glass holders or strings of fairy lights would work well, too.

We've got tiny pom-poms, we've got petrified roses, masks, confetti. It's a PAAARRTTYY!

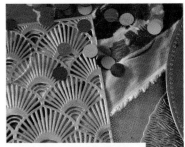

THERE ARE SO MANY DETAILS on this table—not one centerpiece item but a whole array of them. The result? Endless talking points.

CREATIVE ACCENTS

The best way to get guests to relax is to give them something on the table they can grab, use, and share. Here I've set a selection of gorgeous, glittery masks on the table as décor. As the party progresses, someone might even grab a mask and try it on. And why not? The tablescape doesn't have to be a static thing—it can be played with and enjoyed by everyone around the table.

THERE ARE SO MANY different shapes and angles at play on this table. There's no one centerpiece; there are many. The roundness of the paper lanterns and roses contrasts with the angles and points of the star and the metallic feathers and spray.

Nothing has to be completely continuous or organized. You can have your placemats scattered all over the table. There can be one for this place and a different one for that place. Let the base of your table have fun, too!

SIGNATURE DRINK
Aperol Spritz

COLOR SCHEME
Blue and orange

STATEMENT DÉCOR
*Model planes and
fresh flowers*

PLAYLIST
*"Learning to Fly" by
Tom Petty and the
Heartbreakers, "Jetliner"
by Steve Miller Band,
"Fly by Night" by Rush*

TAKE FLIGHT

IF YOU HAVE a lot of blues to incorporate in your design, think blue sky and go with an airy theme that's all about lifting off and being breezy.

CREATIVE ACCENTS

There are so many possible signature drinks with this tablescape. I love an Aperol Spritz, which is orange and bubbly and delightful, but a good G&T with high-quality tonic and some Aviation gin (get it?) makes a perfectly light and approachable cocktail, too. Or go a step further and create "flights" of white wine, cider, or beer for your guests. Small tasting glasses of your favorites will inspire conversation around the table.

*Simple bunches
of carnations are
affordable, frilly,
and fun.*

THE ORANGE ACCENTS really pop against the blue—from the coral placemats to the rose-gold chargers and the bright wings of the biplane.

I've used lighter shades of my main colors throughout, so the pops of pure color from the fresh flowers and planes really draw the eye.

EVERYDAY EXTRAORDINARY

Don't have model planes to incorporate into your tablescape? Fold some of your own! Paper airplanes are so sweet and nostalgic—almost everyone has a memory of folding and flying them. There are lots of different folds to use, from the classic pointed style to more square versions, and they all add wonderful angles and shapes to your table. Bonus if you have some beautiful orange and blue origami paper to use for your mini-planes. And don't be surprised if they're flying around the room by the time dessert rolls around.

SIGNATURE DRINK
Shirley Temple

COLOR SCHEME
Yellow, blue, and pink

STATEMENT DÉCOR
Globe, sunflowers, and text

PLAYLIST
*"With a Little Help from
My Friends" by the Beatles,
"Be Kind" by Marshmello
(with Halsey), "Love
Generation" by Bob Sinclar*

LOVE AND KINDNESS

PURE JOY IN TABLE FORM,
this super-friendly table is perfect
for kids and adults who could
use a little more kindness in their
lives—which, let's be honest, is all
of us. It's a wonderful design for a
birthday party or graduation.

CREATIVE ACCENTS

The best way to show a little
tenderness? Kisses, of course! I
love the foil-wrapped sparkle of a
classic Hershey's Kiss, and it fits
so beautifully with this table. It's
a little treat to snack on before
or after the meal and a fun way
to show affection to your friends
and family.

*Bunching up
your placemats
or runners
creates texture,
and it also
makes natural
folds in which
to nestle flowers.
Here it also
represents waves
of kindness.*

Love
makes the world
BE KIND
Listen

I DON'T KNOW ABOUT YOU, but I show my love with words. I've layered lots of different text elements on this table, from a faux chalkboard to sweet wooden letters to adorable board books at every place setting.

TABLE TIP

The heart napkin fold (see page 44) is one of my all-time favorites. And, as you can see, it's not just for Valentine's Day! Using a patterned napkin, like the striped ones here, gives this fold a trendy, sophisticated feel. Everything on this table is about love and connection. It's an invitation to recognize and appreciate one another.

I value kindness so much. I'd rather
be kind than anything else, so this
table is near and dear to my heart.

FIESTA

TAME ››› WILD!

NEUTRAL ››› COLORFUL

EASY ››› DIFFICULT

SIGNATURE DRINK
Margaritas

COLOR SCHEME
Bright colors of all kinds

STATEMENT DÉCOR
*Sombreros, piñatas,
and maracas*

PLAYLIST
*"La Bamba" by Ritchie
Valens, "Para Siempre"
by Vicente Fernández,
"Besame Mucho" by
Steve Lawrence and
Eydie Gormé, "La Fiesta"
by Will Smith*

MEXICO IS SUCH A vibrant and beautiful place. With a classic fiesta theme, I can show my love for the country. With a party like this, I always make room for the food to share the stage. A build-your-own taco bar is perfect alongside this tablescape.

TABLE TIP

On their own, the piñatas might seem like only a party favor, but they add great energy when you incorporate them into a tablescape with some flowers, a beautiful vase, and a unique centerpiece. When you're shopping, don't think about each item on its own. Rather, picture it woven in with your tablescape.

Miniature maracas add to the fun and can even be snatched up and taken home by guests at the end of the night.

A KNOTTED NAPKIN is visually interesting but couldn't be easier to pull off. Use different color napkins to highlight the variety of colors on the table.

IF YOU'VE GOT margarita glasses on your table, you know you're in for a lively night.

EVERYDAY EXTRAORDINARY

A sombrero with a brim filled with chips is an unexpected and amusing centerpiece. I use colorful balls to add variety to the golden tortilla chips, but you could also use a mix of yellow and blue corn chips to add another color dimension to the presentation. Try placing little bowls of different salsas and guacamole (my favorite!) around the table to create an opportunity for guests to pass and trade salsas.

This is a theme that can be more playful and used for children, or you can elevate it with some gorgeous flowers or an antique vase.

TAME ››› WILD!

NEUTRAL ››› COLORFUL

EASY ››› DIFFICULT

SIGNATURE DRINK
Tea (or a nice Pimm's if you're starting early)

COLOR SCHEME
Bright colors and pastels

STATEMENT DÉCOR
Cats, clocks, and teapots

PLAYLIST
"Happy Pills" by Weathers, "Dance Monkey" by Tones & I, "Mona Lisas and Mad Hatters" by Elton John, "Crazy" by Patsy Cline

MAD HATTER TEA PARTY

THIS FUN AND FRESH take on afternoon tea is great for gathering friends around the table, but it's also extremely child-friendly. It's a natural choice for a birthday party or baby shower.

CREATIVE ACCENTS

Subtle nods to *Alice in Wonderland* pop up all across this tablescape, from ticking clocks to smiling cats and floppy-eared bunnies. Filling fancy teacups and teapots around the table with petrified roses, dyed pampas grass, and other décor defies expectations in a topsy-turvy, Mad Hatter way.

Tying a ruffle around a vase completely transforms it. Now it resembles a fancy tea dress from another era.

An elegant napkin ring removes the need for any fancy folds. When I think afternoon tea, I think fine linens and silver. Although this theme is anything but stuck-up and stuffy, a little polish is never amiss at teatime.

BUGSY ON BOARD

Ever since I was a little kid, I've loved to collect things. In school I earned the nickname "the Scavenger" because I was always looking for things to gather. Rocks, shells . . . whatever it was, I had to collect it. Now I go out and scavenge shops and markets on my travels. I always look for flea markets and the old, tiny, authentic places to shop. It's so satisfying to pick up something that nobody else has, with a story all its own.

SIGNATURE DRINK
Bowl of punch

COLOR SCHEME
Red, white, and bright

STATEMENT DÉCOR
*Popcorn boxes,
tickets, and elephant*

PLAYLIST
*"Tears of a Clown" by the
English Beat, "Tight Rope"
by Leon Russell, "Fire
Eater" by Three Dog Night*

THREE-RING CIRCUS

WHEN YOU'RE AT the circus, you expect to be enchanted and entertained. Do this theme justice with bright pops of color and lots of interactive table elements.

TABLE TIP

For napkins and tableware, you can go with any color scheme, but remember to bring lots of it. The circus is about feeling that childlike wonder. Other elements I've added to evoke that feeling are feathers, colorful pampas grasses, and pom-poms.

I've included real candy lollipops in the theme—you can actually eat your tablescape!

TOP EACH NAPKIN with a single red rose for instant romance and drama.

All you need is one little item to build your design around, whether it's an elephant, a carousel, or even a clown. I've used a couple of rolls of carnival tickets to lift the ceramic elephant off the table.

TABLE TIP

To make it more child-friendly, add soft features, like the pom-poms I've put around the elephant and the beautiful little fluffy drink rings, which you can also use as a way to identify people's drinks while making them look really circusy and clownlike.

PIZZA BAR

TAME ››› WILD!

NEUTRAL ››› COLORFUL

EASY ››› DIFFICULT

SIGNATURE DRINK
Coca-Cola

COLOR SCHEME
Red, white, and black

STATEMENT DÉCOR
Pizza boxes

PLAYLIST
"That's Amore" by Dean Martin, "All Night" by Big Boi, "Let Me Clear My Throat" by DJ Kool

MY TABLESCAPES CAN be very glam, but other times they're meant to be totally casual and relaxed. This Pizza Bar–inspired tablescape is easy-breezy and super fun.

CREATIVE ACCENTS

I made sure to serve Coca-Cola in the signature glasses, because who doesn't love a Coke with pizza? You could just as easily serve cans or classic glass bottles. I love the bright red of the logo and have played off it with the bright red napkins, which I've tied into sweet little packages.

Sometimes you have to think outside the (pizza) box when it comes to creating a fun tablescape.

THE FOOD HERE is the ultimate centerpiece. Giant slices of pizza covered with all the best toppings are a mouth-watering showstopper.

The super-casual vibe is offset by a few refined elements for balance—the pop of blue from a glass vase, a spray of textural flowers, and some woven balls.

THIS CREATIVE CONCEPT can make take-out extra fun at home!

EVERYDAY EXTRAORDINARY

I adore playing with different materials as tablecloths. I've used all kinds of cloth to create interesting bases for my tables, but there's something about the simplicity of newspaper that I just can't get enough of. On this table, the crumpled newspaper tablecloth sets the mood—entertaining, casual, and a little crazy. It adds great texture and lets the bright reds of the table shine.

EVERY ELEMENT should add to the feeling of this being a table at your favorite hole-in-the-wall pizza place.

GLAM

Need some inspiration for creating a one-of-a-kind party that will leave your guests talking? Look no further. These glamorous tablescapes up the ante with deep and bold colors, singular centerpieces, and over-the-top décor. The effect is a unique and alluring mix perfect for an evening where everyone takes it up a notch. The most important part? Be sure to dress like your table! Trust me—you'll have so much fun with these themes.

SIGNATURE DRINK
Circus Rickey

COLOR SCHEME
Gold, red, and blue

STATEMENT DÉCOR
*Spilled popcorn,
pom-poms, and colorful
flowers*

PLAYLIST
*"Disturbia" by Rihanna,
"Circus" by Britney Spears,
"Elephant" by Tame
Impala*

OVER-THE-TOP BIG TOP

LADIES AND GENTLEMEN,
children of all ages, here's a tablescape
your guests will never forget! In this
more grown-up version of a circus
theme, the colors are deeper and
richer, which adds a glamorous feel.

TABLE TIP

This is a really fun theme you can do
at home. It's pretty easy in terms of
finding the items you can put on your
table, because anything goes! Here,
we can easily combine themes: bring
out your red and green Christmas
goblets and throw them into the mix
with gold and silver metallics. Always
remember you can mix and match
elements of any theme to create
something bold and new.

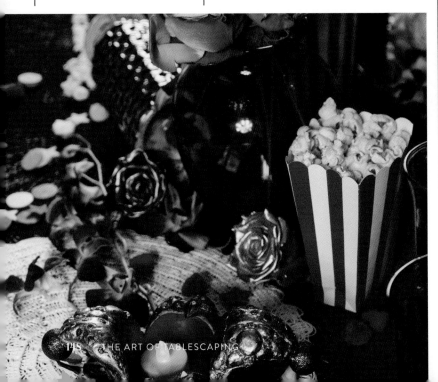

*Sometimes, a
box of popcorn
is all you need
as inspiration
for a color story!*

ONCE AGAIN, I look like my table. We are doing a three-ring circus, and here I am: the ringleader of the tablescape! Take it over the big top with your outfits *and* your décor!

Tablescapes are about having fun and being happy, so use whatever makes you feel happy—especially in this glam circus theme! If you find something in your house that is playful but doesn't perfectly fit the theme, throw it on there anyway. A circus is not supposed to make sense!

CREATIVE ACCENTS

Creating texture on your table is as easy as popping microwave popcorn! Filling a beautiful vase with popcorn and artfully toppling it over adds tons of character to this circus theme. Confetti and colorful pom-poms strewn about also create texture. I used the threaded pom-poms as a path for the eye to travel as it moves around the table.

TAME »»» WILD!

NEUTRAL »»» COLORFUL

EASY »»» DIFFICULT

SIGNATURE DRINK
*Rioja or another
Spanish red wine*

COLOR SCHEME
Red, orange, and gold

STATEMENT DÉCOR
*Bull, lace parasol,
and cigar boxes*

PLAYLIST
*"Despacito" by Luis Fonsi,
"La Malagueña" by Juan
Martín, "La Bomba" by
Ricky Martin*

SPANISH TAPAS

WELCOME TO SPAIN! This super-simple but super-beautiful tapas theme is perfect if you and your guests just want to have a few finger foods and a glass of wine.

TABLE TIP

The great thing about a setup like this is that it's very easy to throw together and very versatile—just like tapas themselves. It's the perfect theme if you're having a couple of friends over. The lush tones and fresh flowers add some romance to the table, too, so it can set the mood for a romantic date. This Spanish-themed table draws on the reds and golds from the Spanish flag, complemented with burnt orange.

I could have set this table with a floral arrangement in the middle, but I'm not conventional in that sense whatsoever. My primary item in this 'scape is the Spanish bull. I just love him!

NOTICE HOW I'M working with height here. The glassware and flower arrangements draw your eye up, while the cigar boxes, dried blood orange, and gladiolas strewn on the table draw your eye down.

CREATIVE ACCENTS

This sweet little parasol is the secondary item of my centerpiece, and I just adore it. The lace reminds me of a flamenco fan or the mantilla of a Spanish dancer. By flipping the umbrella upside down, I was able to toss in some wooden and fabric balls, which add even more texture and a pop of color. The parasol offers a nice contrast and a chance to continue the Spanish-themed story in a new way on the table.

THE RED COOKIE TINS fit in perfectly with my color story, even though they come from Italy. The mood is the most important thing here.

*Napkins are always
a festive part of the
tablescape. Because
this 'scape is Spanish
inspired and the color
theme throughout the
table is red with a little
bit of burnt orange, I've
decided to go with this
rose napkin. I think
it works beautifully
with the theme. And
though it looks super
elegant, the rose fold is
very simple to do. (See
page 46.)*

TAME ⟫⟫ WILL!

NEUTRAL ⟫⟫ COLORFUL

EASY ⟫⟫ DIFFICULT

SIGNATURE DRINK
Jellab

COLOR SCHEME
Rose gold, oranges, reds, and everything else!

STATEMENT DÉCOR
Bruce the camel, Aladdin-inspired decanter, and an antique teapot

PLAYLIST
"Aleb" by Yasmine Hamdan, "Mafi Mennik" by Aziz Maraka, "Ya Nassini" by Elias Rahbani, "Arabian Nights" by Will Smith

ARABIAN NIGHTS

HERE'S A TABLE that creates such an enticing vibe and so much ambiance. Add some delicious Middle Eastern food, and you'll have a magical evening.

TABLE TIP

Really push your creativity. I have so much fun with themes like this one because I'm obsessed with color and I'm all about mixing and matching different kinds of objects. Just as in a bazaar, there's a lot of different elements here: We have fresh flowers, wicker balls, and pink grasses. We've got gorgeous greens, reds, pinks, and purples. Find themes that let you put everything on the table!

I've used rose-gold chargers with this setup to highlight the oranges, pinks, and reds throughout the table. They really tie everything together.

LOOK AT THIS amazing *Aladdin*-inspired decanter that I found at a thrift shop. It came with little cups, too, which are beautiful. I just love thrift shops!

CREATIVE ACCENTS

Mix it up! In this setting, I've mixed the glasses. I've got the same theme on the small glasses going all the way through. But I've also used different kinds of wine and water glasses. There are greens and yellows, just to make it fun and a bit different. Mixed glassware is a great conversation starter, because it's something guests will notice and something that will get them talking.

AS PART OF THE centerpiece, you'll see the decorative camel. We named him Bruce. He's a beautiful antique, and he has so much texture and character. He's obviously got an old story, which I love, because he brings that talking point to the table.

I've incorporated two different table runners in this 'scape. They're completely different colors but they're both a similar style. Then, I've used matching placemats all the way through. The effect adds a lot of color but also something consistent for the eye. I love these placemats because they have tassels, which fits perfectly with the Arabian Nights theme—anything with tassels, beads, or little gemstones all over works here.

SIGNATURE DRINK

Rum Runner

COLOR SCHEME

Red, gold, and black

STATEMENT DÉCOR

*Doubloons,
petrified roses,
and mask*

PLAYLIST

*"Chasing Pirates" by
Norah Jones, "Jolly Roger
(Remastered)" by Adam
& the Ants, "Banshee" by
Young Dubliners*

PIRATE GOLD

PICTURE THE TABLE of a pirate queen, one who's ready to celebrate an especially good haul. Her table must be dripping in gold, from the plates she'll eat off to the pile of treasure in the center of the table to the handfuls of coins strewn about. In other words, gilded to the gills and with over-the-top opulence.

CREATIVE ACCENTS

Whatever drink you serve, make sure you do it in a goblet. The ruby-red goblets here are just what I imagine a pirate captain holding in one hand, feet up on the table after a day of plundering. A rich red wine fills them nicely—but remember that pirates are known for their love of rum.

A well-placed golden skull, black feathers, and red tulle unmistakably say "pirate."

THERE ARE SO MANY different textures of gold on this table—it's a feast for the eyes. From the round chargers and the tiny gold squares on the tablecloth to the hammered gold vessels, the doubloons, and of course the elegant petrified roses.

BUGSY ON BOARD

I have been known to dress up as "Chief Pirate"—complete with braided beard and eye patch—to serve lunch to guests on a yacht. I'm very good at reading the room, and if the guest experience would be enhanced by a full-on piratical display, I will gladly don the required costume. For this glam pirate 'scape, I've kept it a little more refined with this saucy mask, but don't be afraid to sneak some costume elements into your spread should your guests be inclined to let loose themselves.

I BOUGHT a few yards of this stunning gold-striped cloth for a table covering and just laid it down, raw edges and all. The unfinished edges help it perfectly walk that line between luxe-and-glam and rough-and-ready, just what you'd expect from a pirate feast.

These little boat vessels echo the design of the gold chargers and easily hold a variety of textural flowers to create height and drama.

SIGNATURE DRINK
Old-Fashioned

COLOR SCHEME
Gold, silver, and blue

STATEMENT DÉCOR
1920s car, alcohol bottles, pearls, pearls, and more pearls

PLAYLIST
"A Little Party Never Killed Nobody" by Fergie, "Miss Fisher's Theme" by Greg J Walker, "Bang Bang" by will.i.am

TOTALLY GLAM GATSBY

GATSBY IS MY ultimate theme! Inspired by the classic novel *The Great Gatsby* and dripping with decadence, this versatile theme works for birthday parties and an elevated New Year's Eve bash.

CREATIVE ACCENTS

Just like the Roaring '20s, this table is high-spirited! I've incorporated different bottles of alcohol—whiskey, tequila, gin, anything from your bar—as a nod to Prohibition and to create different heights around the table. Because Gatsby is opulent and super extravagant, we've got tons of glitter, pearls, and silver and gold here, with blue as an accent. Picturing Gatsby and his beloved Daisy, I've set this as a table for two. But you can easily expand this for more guests.

I've used a lot of pearls to create the texture on the table. Spilling out of jewelry boxes, wrapped around bottles, dripping over the décor. Isn't it glamorous?

DO I BLEND IN with this glam table? Have fun dressing to this theme. A black off-the-shoulder number and feathery fascinator in your hair create a playful flapper look. Don't forget the pearls!

NOTICE THE BEAUTIFUL grass leaves. They look like feathers, but I think they're a little more creative. The natural elements of the grasses and petrified roses balance out the sparkly, glittery elements of the table.

I bought this beautiful blue car at a thrift shop. It just happened to be there, and it was so perfect for this 'scape. More often than not, I find excellent pieces while casually browsing. So whenever you find yourself in a shop, staring at the perfect centerpiece that you know one day will look amazing on a table, just pick it up!

TABLE TIP

Looking at everything together, you can see how the different heights draw your eye across the table, and how everything is linked by those strands of pearls. I also ran tulle all the way through. I've even thrown a random shoe into the mix, because what better way to up the ante than with a shoe on the table! At the end of the party, after dancing all night and enjoying way too much champagne, your guests just might kick off their shoes, too!

HOLIDAY

I just love holidays. You and your loved ones gather around the table to share a meal, conversation, and time. What's more perfect than that? But remember: just because holidays have iconic imagery and classic color schemes doesn't mean you have to incorporate them into your décor. In fact, adding a twist to your holiday tablescape themes is the perfect way to create new and lasting memories for you and your loved ones.

TAME ››› WILD!

NEUTRAL ››› COLORFUL

EASY ››› DIFFICULT

SIGNATURE DRINK
Dark and Stormy

COLOR SCHEME
*Black, dark green,
purple, and orange*

STATEMENT DÉCOR
*Velvet pumpkins, skull,
and dark foliage*

PLAYLIST
*"Thriller" by Michael
Jackson, "Bela Lugosi's
Dead" by Bauhaus, "Psycho
Killer" by Talking Heads*

SPOOKY AND glamorous, this table evokes the feeling of stepping out into a misty night in late fall, where the only light is from a full moon. It's giving off major Halloween vibes, but there's nothing kitschy about it thanks to the blacks, greens, dark purples, and mauve.

CREATIVE ACCENTS

I've used tons of textural foliage here—some real, some cloth. High-end fake flowers and leaves can be found at most craft and fabric stores. They're easy to store and a wonderful alternative to fresh botanicals, especially in the late autumn and winter. Even more, their stems are bendable and it is easy to manipulate their shape.

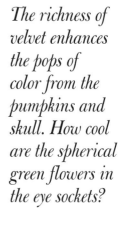

The richness of velvet enhances the pops of color from the pumpkins and skull. How cool are the spherical green flowers in the eye sockets?

THE LANTERN, candle, pumpkin, and skull make me think of "The Legend of Sleepy Hollow"—take your inspiration from a classic ghost story, then ask guests to retell some of their favorites around the table.

TABLE TIP

You've probably noticed versions of this placemat throughout my 'scapes—I love this design, so I have them in virtually every color. Layering two organic tones—in this case light green and brown/black—brings to mind the deep woods, filled with lichen, mosses, and spiderwebs. The green lower mat ties into the colors of the vines and pumpkins.

SINCE I'M THE QUEEN of Theme, of course I have spiderweb napkins and bat napkin rings. But I think it's the black cloth fern frond that really amplifies the spookiness of this table setting.

The dark colors bring the drama and the glamor, but the hints of orange and gold keep it fun and light—I've got the lantern, the glittery candle, the orange pumpkin, and of course the table runner.

TAME ››› WILL!

NEUTRAL ››› COLORFUL

EASY ››› DIFFICULT

SIGNATURE DRINK

Blood Orange Paloma

COLOR SCHEME

Deep maroon, bone white, and bold, vivid accent colors

STATEMENT DÉCOR

Flower crown, decorative skulls, and bright flowers

PLAYLIST

"Calaveritas" by Ana Tijoux, "La Bruja" by Dan Zanes, "El Son de la Negra" by Mariachi Vargas de Tecalitlán

DÍA DE LOS MUERTOS

A HOLIDAY FULL OF symbolism and meaning, the Mexican Day of the Dead is a celebration of life as much as death—and an explosion of color.

CREATIVE ACCENTS

Iconic decorative Day of the Dead sugar skulls are traditionally given as offerings during the Mexican holiday. Here, these replicas double as sweet, vibrant décor for your table. To tie things together, pick a few colors from each skull and use those colors in your table's foundation.

Using a uniform color for certain elements in an exuberant theme like this one helps tie everything together. Here, I've used a gorgeous deep maroon for the napkins and glasses.

MARIGOLDS AND GLADIOLAS are symbolic flowers used in Day of the Dead celebrations and are sometimes woven into crowns. This paper version doubles as a radiant and meaningful centerpiece.

With colors as vivid as the skulls I've used as inspiration here, you can really push the boundaries of your décor. These otherworldly blue-and-purple orchids are just the right touch.

TABLE TIP

Because the skulls are so colorful, I've opted to use just a table runner and simple folded placemats in this setup rather than additional tablecloths. The clean lines of the table give the eye some negative space before it focuses on the explosion of beautiful colors in the middle of the table. Folding the placemats and draping the tassels off the table adds some unexpected fun, too.

TAME »» WILD!

NEUTRAL »» COLORFUL

EASY »» DIFFICULT

SIGNATURE DRINK
Apple Cider Mimosa

COLOR SCHEME
Silver, blue, and green

STATEMENT DÉCOR
*Velvet pumpkin, golden
grasses, and tulle*

PLAYLIST
*"Thankful" by Kelly
Clarkson, "Grateful" by
Rita Ora, "Thank You"
by Chris Cornell*

THANKSGIVING WITH A TWIST

HERE'S A THANKSGIVING

table for the whole family. Playing
with themes of thanks and plenty,
this classy tablescape will take your
turkey up a notch.

TABLE TIP

Always look for ways to incorporate
flowers—fresh-cut and dried—into
your tablescapes. It brings a bit
of nature to your table to balance
out the other elements. In the fall
and winter months, dried grasses
and petrified roses are a must.
In this case, the grasses nicely
complement the pumpkin décor
and are a neat addition.

*Arrangements are
a great place to
play with texture.
Wrapping botanical
arrangements in
tulle combines the soft
sparkle of the fabric
with the spiked tips
of the dried grass.
It's a sophisticated
addition to your
table.*

NEVER BE AFRAID to mix your metallics. The silver pear and pumpkin centerpiece elements, gold chargers, silver napkin rings, and sparkling golden glass pebbles together make for a dazzling effect.

EVERYDAY EXTRAORDINARY

Always look for ways to surprise your guests with unexpected elements. Here again, I've turned things on their heads! This simple technique of filling a wine glass with tulle and an interesting detail—in this case, a dried thistle—then flipping it over works time and time again. Adding a tea light or flameless candle on top adds instant ambiance.

I JUST LOVE this green *Shrek* pumpkin centerpiece! It's an iconic fall item with a twist—the velvety, vibrant green and the silvery stem. It's classic with a bit of bling!

Aren't these metallic pumpkins and pears fabulous? When you're shopping or thrifting, always keep an eye out for usual items done unusually. These silver pears allowed me to take this 'scape to another place!

SIGNATURE DRINK
Pink Peppercorn Gimlet

COLOR SCHEME
Pink, gold, and wood

STATEMENT DÉCOR
*Metallic and woven
pumpkins and balls*

PLAYLIST
*"I've Got Plenty to Be
Thankful For" by Bing
Crosby, "Danke Schoen"
by Wayne Newton,
"Thanksgiving Song" by
Mary Chapin Carpenter*

THANKSGIVING IN PINK

WHOEVER SAID you have to have a cornucopia on your table to mark Thanksgiving? Sweet and gentle on the eyes, this fresh, rosy take on the holiday offers a charming alternative.

CREATIVE ACCENTS

You can see I've peppered this table with items that are reminiscent of seasonal décor without going full-on autumnal. Sometimes a suggestion of your theme can be more powerful (and more refined) than saying it outright. To create that energy, I've used round, gourd-like shapes; a crystalline pumpkin straight out of "Cinderella"; and a woven centerpiece that is soft and feminine but instantly recalls an autumn harvest.

I'm not American, but I love the tradition of gathering around a table to express gratitude for life, family, and friends.

NATURAL, ORGANIC REMINDERS of fall—pinecones, dried flowers, and dehydrated citrus—add texture to the table. Their muted colors are grounding to the bright pinks and layered metallics.

TABLE TIP

Remember, contrasting shapes and textures add visual interest. In this design, I love the way the round, two-toned gold chargers and plates are offset by the pure pink triangular napkins. This fold is as simple as can be. Take a square napkin, fold it in half to form a rectangle, in half again to form a square, and in half a third time to form a triangle. Then pull one corner of the triangle back to touch the long edge.

THE SOFT WATERCOLOR design on the tablecloth pulls the eye toward the structural, textural elements at the center of the table.

Like my table, my outfit is soft and muted with pops of bright color and metallics—eyes, lips, clips, and earrings, of course.

GOLDEN HARVEST THANKSGIVING

TABLES LIKE THIS, rich with orange and gold, have a place all over the world. Even if you don't celebrate Thanksgiving, you can come together with friends and family to raise a glass to the bounty of the harvest, the waning days of autumn, and the light you'll keep burning bright throughout the dark winter months.

TABLE TIP

Light up! Notice how the strings of fairy lights illuminate different facets of the glass vases, the undersides of the pumpkins and ornamental corn, and the glittery décor and glass pebbles spaced around the table. They draw your eye to different elements of the 'scape, but also pull everything together into a cohesive whole.

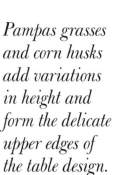

*Pampas grasses
and corn husks
add variations
in height and
form the delicate
upper edges of
the table design.*

SPIKY AND SOFT, glitzy and natural—the contrasting elements here are united by using consistently warm colors across the whole table.

CREATIVE ACCENTS

After a long and luxurious meal around this glittering table, consider serving a digestif to wind things down and close out the meal. A classic herbal liqueur, such as Fernet-Branca or Amaro, would pair nicely with the colors and botanicals on this table—or, for that matter, a warm, golden-hued spirit like a brandy or an aged Scotch. For a non-alcoholic option, consider a warming ginger or turmeric tea.

I'VE LAID A SCATTERING of fall leaves across the simple napkin in the center of the bronze charger plate to introduce more of that natural element.

*The lighting
and atmosphere
of the room
really contribute
to this table's
success. Warm,
soft lights are key.*

HAPPY HANUKKAH

TAME ››› WILD!

NEUTRAL ››› COLORFUL

EASY ››› DIFFICULT

SIGNATURE DRINK
Hot Chocolate Gelt Cocktail

COLOR SCHEME
Blue, silver, white, and gold

STATEMENT DÉCOR
*Menorah, white roses,
and chocolate gelt*

PLAYLIST
*"8 Days (of Hanukkah)"
by Sharon Jones & the
Dap-Kings, "Hanukkah
Dance," by Woody Guthrie,
"Hanukkah on Japonica"
by Panorama Jazz Band*

BEAUTIFUL CANDLELIGHT
and traditional holiday colors
are all the inspiration you need
to create a warm and inviting
tablescape for Hanukkah.

CREATIVE ACCENTS

I just love the way the candlelight from the menorah plays
off the metallics and glassware
on the table. The gold of the
chocolate gelt coins looks
warmer, and the silver accents
sparkle. When you're incorporating candlelight into your
tablescape—especially as the
centerpiece—think about how
your other décor can reflect
that light back to your guests.

*Using simple,
clear wine
glasses in this
tablescape
allows the
other elements
to stand out.*

Hanukkah gelt— foil-wrapped chocolate coins—are traditionally given to children during this holiday. By incorporating them into the table, I've added another shining element to reflect candlelight— and guests can take them home at the end of the evening.

TABLE TIP

White roses add a simple elegance to any table. By pairing them with painted or dyed dried flowers in a single complementary hue, like the deep-blue blossoms here, you can create breathtaking arrangements.

TAME »» WILD!

NEUTRAL »» COLORFUL

EASY »» DIFFICULT

SIGNATURE DRINK
Eggnog

COLOR SCHEME
White, red, and green

STATEMENT DÉCOR
*Gift-wrapped boxes,
red votive candles,
and holiday characters*

PLAYLIST
*"White Christmas" by
Bing Crosby, "Silver and
Gold" by Burl Ives, "I Saw
Mommy Kissing Santa
Claus" by the Ronettes*

WHITE CHRISTMAS

EVEN IF YOU LIVE somewhere warm, you can still set your holiday table with snow-dusted evergreens in mind. This holiday 'scape has a very north-woods quality going for it—cozy and intimate.

EVERYDAY EXTRAORDINARY

Christmas tree ornaments aren't just for the tree—they are perfect for table décor, shiny, festive, and evocative. Use them as freestanding objects or mix them into a glass vase with some foliage. You could even place a unique ornament at each table setting, giving your guests something to identify their places and spark conversations.

A few special holiday characters have chosen to make this table their home. My silver stags and this little gnome—called a tomte *or* nisse *in Scandinavia— bring a sweet friendliness to the 'scape.*

PULL SOME OF THE central décor off the table when it's time to eat and lay large platters down for a family-style meal. Soon you'll be passing trays of food and sharing with your neighbors.

INCORPORATE THE SPACE beyond your table into your tablescape—hang décor on the walls to make your whole room party ready.

Dashing through the Snow with a bottle of Merlot

CREATIVE ACCENTS

Gift-wrapped boxes make for a festive centerpiece. Wrap a few of different sizes and stack them haphazardly—like a pile of presents under the tree. You could even remove the top of one, set a napkin inside, and use it as a breadbasket.

Mixing metallics—silver and gold!—is perfect for a holiday theme.

TAME »» WILD!

NEUTRAL »» COLORFUL

EASY »» DIFFICULT

SIGNATURE DRINK
Mulled wine

COLOR SCHEME
Red, green, and gold

STATEMENT DÉCOR
*Foliage, gift-wrapped boxes,
and holiday crackers*

PLAYLIST
*"Have Yourself a Merry
Little Christmas" by
Michael Bublé, "Winter
Song" by Leslie Odom
Junior, "Here Comes Santa
Claus" by Gene Autry*

CLASSIC CHRISTMAS

MAKE HOLIDAY MAGIC with this tablescape. It's formal, fancy, and oh so chic.

TABLE TIP

Nothing is more beautiful than a candlelit table. Real or fake, the soft, glowing light of a votive makes everyone look good— and elevates the table's décor. You'll want to avoid scented candles, however, lest they interfere with the smell of your delicious meal (or happen to be a scent that one of your guests just can't stand).

Red and green flowers and foliage are easy to source, even in the winter— though in a pinch you can always grab a few fake sprigs from a craft store.

LAYER YOUR PLACE SETTINGS with colorful chargers and luxurious red napkins. Fill your table with bright and brilliant golds, and don't forget to add hints of sparkle where you can!

BUGSY ON BOARD

Holiday crackers are a wonderful tradition that make for a fun activity and icebreaker. We always had them when I was growing up in South Africa. Placed one to a plate, they look like gift-wrapped presents for your guests. Traditionally, you cross arms and grasp one end of your cracker and one end of the cracker belonging to the neighbor to your left. When everyone is ready, the whole table pulls at once and the crackers should pop open, revealing fun prizes, paper crowns, and jokes or riddles for the table to share.

Feel free to mix and match table linens and napkins, even on a busy table like this. As long as you are referencing your central color theme, you can have fun with different patterns.

SIGNATURE DRINK

Holiday sangria

COLOR SCHEME

Red, gold, and blue

STATEMENT DÉCOR

*Moroccan-inspired table
runner, evergreen branches,
and Christmas ornaments*

PLAYLIST

*"Mele Kalikimaka" by She
& Him, "Little Drummer
Boy/Peace on Earth" by
David Bowie and Bing
Crosby, "At the Christmas
Ball" by Bessie Smith*

WARM CHRISTMAS

INSTEAD OF HAVING a white Christmas, what if it's a warm Christmas? This tablescape blends traditional colors and themes with new ideas.

BUGSY ON BOARD

Growing up in South Africa, below the equator, for me, Christmas came in the summertime. So I can't resist weaving warm colors into my holiday tablescapes. It's a great change of pace from the usual red, green, and white. In this 'scape, I was inspired by the warm colors and gorgeous textures I experienced traveling through Morocco. So the décor is evocative of warm, vibrant places.

Pair iconic holiday items with unexpected details. Evergreen stems and holiday plaid pair surprisingly well with warm Moroccan tones, dried lemons, and pottery.

FLAMELESS CANDLES are a perfect option for closely nestled arrangements like this one.

I do love my napkin folds, but sometimes a simple napkin ring is just the right detail. Here, the napkin ring visually echoes the texture of the wicker balls.

EVERYDAY EXTRAORDINARY

Sure, the top of your table runner is gorgeous. But check out the underside, too. For this tablescape, I flipped the runner upside down, then folded the ends over at an angle. It allowed me to highlight the red foundation in the centerpiece and added beautiful detail under the place settings.

RESOURCES

SHOPPING FOR YOUR TABLE

Shopping for your table is one part intention, one part luck. I have my go-to shops for when I know I need to pick up a specific item for a table, and I always keep my eye out when I'm in those stores for little inspiring pieces of décor that I can snag and tuck away for later use. The other part of shopping for me is just being out and about and making sure my tablescape brain is always turned on. You never know when a perfect future centerpiece will call your name!

WHERE TO SHOP

I spend a lot of time in craft and fabric stores. I find them to be so inspiring. Just walking in the door gives me ideas! They're a great place to buy items in bulk. I visit a florist for fresh flowers—or pluck them from my garden. Meanwhile, thrift stores are probably my favorite resource for exciting and unique centerpiece objects, but I also love to keep my eye out for one-of-a-kind items during my travels. I have been known to purchase an extra suitcase on my way home for packing and transporting any newly found treasures I picked up while in one port or another. And every now and again, when I need a really specific item, online retailers can save the day.

WHAT TO LOOK FOR

When you're wandering through a store with your mind on tablescaping, think about what you need—but also keep your mind open to inspiration.

MY GO-TO CRAFT STORE BUYS:
- Glass pebbles
- Tulle
- Candles and candleholders
- Fabric flowers and leaves

WHEN TRAVELING THE WORLD, I KEEP MY EYE OUT FOR:
- Objects that evoke a specific place
- Handmade fabrics and pottery

WHEN I'M IN A THRIFT SHOP, I LOOK FOR:
- Fun, beautiful, or interesting statuettes
- Vintage glassware, vases, or serving platters
- Wicker baskets
- Ceramics
- Antique metal vases (a quick polish usually removes any discoloration)
- Costume jewelry to drape around a table

MAKING THE BEST USE OF SALES

I'm always ready to pounce on a good deal for the sake of my 'scapes. Here's what I keep in mind as I shop:

- Find a placemat or tablecloth you like that's on sale? Buy it in multiple colors so that you have options for layering your table while maintaining a cohesive design.
- Think about your storage situation. Are you buying a load of new napkins? Make sure you pick up the necessary storage items to be able to put away the linens when you get home. See page 212 for tips. No one wants to find a forgotten bag of wrinkled linens in the back of the closet a few weeks after a shopping trip.
- Shop for seasonal décor just after the holiday in question for the best discounts, then store until the next season. Look for classic design sensibilities—you don't want to buy something that's trendy now but will look dated in a year.

SETTING A BUDGET

So, if you're always on the lookout for great décor, how do you set—or stay within—a budget? For me, it's all about deciding what's essential and what's not. Here are some tips:

- Set a monthly budget for essential design items for your 'scapes. If you blow it all on ten different colors of placemats, then you might have to wait until next month to stock up on candles; use your LED tea lights for your next event.
- If you're overbudget but your table décor isn't quite what you want it to be, reach out to friends or search your home for items you can repurpose. Necessity is the mother of invention, after all!
- Keep a rainy-day fund for those truly unique thrift store finds. You can score lots of good deals shopping thrift or consignment, and it's worth it to have some just-for-fun décor that no one will have seen before.

- If you find a really stunning item you absolutely must have for an upcoming or future table, consider the quality of the item and its staying power. Don't get it just because it's trendy— make sure it is well made, can be repurposed for a lot of different looks, and won't be outdated in a few months.
- Channel your budget into must-have items. No table runner? That's OK; maybe there's an everyday item you can make extraordinary. But no glassware? That could be a big problem!

REPURPOSING

You've probably noticed some of the same statement items and supporting décor showing up in my signature 'scapes. I make it a point to find and purchase materials I know will find new life on table after table. A spiky ball can be a sea urchin or an exploding firework; a wicker or rattan ball can complement a casual outdoor lunch or an elegant evening dinner. Here are some tips for reusing your décor:

- Choose versatility with your essential items. Think simple napkins in a few warm and cool colors, a wide variety of the same basic type of runner or placemat for layering, or neutrals that go with everything.
- Invest in a few large glass vases in various shapes that can be filled with different items and transformed depending on your event.
- Use the same items in different themes by pairing them with various colors and textures, turning them on their sides, or revealing another angle.
- Add something to an item to transform it—raise it up to a different level, surround it with lights, or drape it with strings of beads.

STORAGE

A tidy storage system is simply a must for your 'scaping supplies. With a little forethought and planning, all of your materials will be at your fingertips the next time you're hosting a get-together.

ORGANIZATION AND LABELING

How will you categorize your tablescaping supplies? And how will you label them? Do your future self a favor and carefully and systematically categorize, store, and label your items for later use.

ORGANIZING

Consider the objects that belong exclusively to a certain theme—for example, a specific holiday—and objects that you reuse again and again. I group some items by theme and others by function. Storing themed holiday supplies together is a no-brainer. I'm not going to use a miniature Christmas gnome for many other parties. But other supplies—strings of lights, small containers with glitter of different shapes and sizes, vases, fake flowers and leaves, collections of wicker balls—are easier to find when they are grouped together.

LABELING

Don't forget to label any containers you're using. And the more detail you can include, the better. Trust me, you'll thank yourself later. I often include a general label—for example, "lighting"—with a sub-label telling me exactly what's in the bin, such as "electric tea lights and votives." That way I don't have to dig through all of my "lighting" bins to find what I need.

THE BEST WAYS TO STORE DÉCOR

Depending on the décor, your best bet is to store your items either in containers with lids or on hangers.

CONTAINERS

I like to keep the bulk of my décor in plastic bins. They're stackable, and you can see at a glance what's inside. Plus they're easy to label. But boxes will do, too. Just keep in mind where you're storing your materials. If you're putting your containers in a basement or another area that's subject to moisture, think about using a more protective container. Make sure all of your materials are clean and dry before storing them, and bear in mind that some delicate items will need to be wrapped in tissue or Bubble Wrap for protection.

HANGERS

For table linens, storing on hangers is the best way to keep stubborn wrinkles and creases from becoming an issue right before your event. If you can set aside a devoted closet space or portable hanging rack for your table linens, you can save yourself a lot of hassle. As with other items, be aware of whether your storage space is susceptible to moisture (lest they become moldy).

STORING CLOTH

You know what's the worst? Pulling out a bin of linens and realizing that some are still dirty or that the whole batch is hopelessly wrinkled and requires a steaming to get party ready. Follow these tips to make sure your cloth items are ready for showtime when you are.

- Wash immediately after the party—like, the night of!
- Iron flat after drying.
- Consider storing napkins flat in a large square container. If you can't do that, fold in half, then into thirds, and store in neat stacks.
- Store matching napkins together by color and texture.
- Store runners and tablecloths folded neatly and draped over wooden hangers. Check periodically to make sure they are still properly in place.
- Store placemats on hangers. If they're a heavy material, consider hanging them in small batches by clips. If they're softer cloth, fold once and hang over the bar of a wooden hanger.

STORING BREAKABLES

Obviously, you're not going to just toss a crystal vase into a bin, but consider the durability of all of your décor when you're storing it.

- Vases, glassware, and ceramics should be wrapped with tissue or Bubble Wrap and packed into solid bins with enough headroom in the bins that they can be stacked without placing pressure on the objects.
- Some items might not be breakable, but they can be bent out of shape. Delicate metals or wicker items are easy to accidentally damage. Store them individually or with like items, again making sure they are not packed too tightly.

CHECKLISTS & PROMPTS

PLANNING YOUR PARTY CHECKLIST

Here are some lists to help you think through your options for table essentials, centerpieces, supporting décor, and fun extras. Grab one of each, or throw as many as you like on the table if the occasion allows!

TABLE ESSENTIALS

Crockery

- ○ Porcelain
- ○ Ceramic
- ○ Wooden boards
- ○ Slate

Cutlery

- ○ Stainless steel
- ○ Silver, gold, or copper
- ○ Colorful acrylic
- ○ Chopsticks

Glassware

- ○ Colorful goblets
- ○ Crystal stemware
- ○ Stemless glasses
- ○ Acrylic tumblers

Napkins

- ○ Paper
- ○ Cotton
- ○ Linen
- ○ Silk

CENTERPIECES

- ○ Statues
- ○ Objets d'art
- ○ Vases
- ○ Pillar candles

- ○ Fresh flowers
- ○ Dried flowers
- ○ Lighting

FOUNDATION ITEMS

Tablecloths

- Linen
- Satin/silk
- Patterned
- Burlap
- Butcher paper
- Newspaper
- Netting

Runners

- Embroidered
- Woven
- Macramé
- Paper

Placemats

- Round
- Rectangular
- Woven
- Rough

Chargers

- Silver
- Gold
- Bronze

SUPPORTING DÉCOR

Textured items

- Plants, flowers, and other botanicals
- Cloth
- Wicker or rattan
- Glass
- Metal

Round shapes

- Plates
- Chargers
- Vases
- Candles
- Platters
- Cake stands
- Round placemats

Angular shapes

- Grasses
- Stars
- Crystals
- Square or rectangular placemats
- Table runners

High points

- Elevated centerpieces
- Grasses
- Feathers
- Large flower arrangements
- Large votive candles

Low objects

- Individual flowers
- Small collections of rattan or wicker balls
- Tea lights

BLING AND SPARKLE

Lighting

- ○ Flameless candles
- ○ Wax candles
- ○ Fairy lights
- ○ Lamps
- ○ Lanterns

Sparkle and extras

- ○ Glitter
- ○ Costume jewelry
- ○ Glass
- ○ Crystal
- ○ Metallic items

- ○ Small figurines and other objects

ATMOSPHERE

Drinks

- ○ Cocktails
- ○ Mocktails
- ○ Wine
- ○ Water
- ○ Sparkling water

Playlist

- ○ Classics
- ○ Contemporary
- ○ Instrumental

Attire

- ○ Outfit
- ○ Jewelry
- ○ Other accessories
- ○ Makeup

THEME NAME

TAME ››› WILD!

NEUTRAL ››› COLORFUL

EASY ››› DIFFICULT

SIGNATURE DRINK

COLOR SCHEME

STATEMENT DÉCOR

PLAYLIST

[FILL IN THE BLANK] INSPIRATION

CELEBRATING A PERSON

This is a celebration of _____. We first met
person

at _____. I instantly noticed their
place

personality was _____ and _____. My
adjective   _adjective_

favorite thing about them is _____. If there's
noun

one thing I want everyone to know about them, it's that

they are _____. When they see _____,
adjective or noun   _noun_

they absolutely light up. The colors I associate with this

person are _____, _____, and _____.
color   _color_   _color_

*Write down one
memory about this
person that you'd like
to incorporate into
your décor:*

[FILL IN THE BLANK] INSPIRATION

CELEBRATING A HOLIDAY OR OCCASION

This event will celebrate _____. When I
holiday or occasion

think about this holiday/occasion, I feel _____
feeling

and _____. To me, these things are
feeling

emblematic of this holiday: _____,
noun

_____, _____, and
noun *noun*

_____. Words I want my guests to use
noun

to describe this event are _____,
adjective

_____, and _____.
adjective *adjective*

The colors I associate with this holiday occasion are

_____, _____,
color *color*

and _____.
color

*Write down something you
love about this holiday that
you'd like to incorporate
into your décor:*

THEME NAME

TAME ››› WILD!
————————————

NEUTRAL ››› COLORFUL
————————————

EASY ››› DIFFICULT
————————————

SIGNATURE DRINK

COLOR SCHEME

STATEMENT DÉCOR

PLAYLIST

[FILL IN THE BLANK] INSPIRATION

THEME NAME

TAME ››› WILD!

NEUTRAL ››› COLORFUL

EASY ››› DIFFICULT

SIGNATURE DRINK

COLOR SCHEME

STATEMENT DÉCOR

PLAYLIST

CELEBRATING A SPECIAL TIME PERIOD

At this event, we'll travel back in time to _____.
time period

People at that time wore _____ and
clothing item

_____, and if you lived at that time, you might own
clothing item

a _____ or a _____. Drinks
noun   *noun*

and food I associate with that time include _____
food/drink

and _____. The colors that come to mind
food/drink

when I think of that era include _____, _____,
color   *color*

and _____, and when people remember it, they
color

think about _____ and _____.
person/event   *person/event*

Words that are often used to describe that time period

include _____, _____,
adjective   *adjective*

and _____.
adjective

Write down one inspiration from this time period that you'd like to incorporate into your décor:

[FILL IN THE BLANK] INSPIRATION

CELEBRATING A FAVORITE PLACE

This event celebrates one of my favorite places,

_____. When I close my eyes and picture
favorite place

it, I see _____, _____, and
noun *noun*

_____. The most common colors there are
noun

_____, _____, and _____.
color *color* *color*

If I were there right now, the air around me would be

_____, so I would be wearing _____.
temperature *outfit*

The foods and drinks I most associate with _____
place

are _____ and _____. When I'm
food/drink *food/drink*

there, I feel _____.
feeling

*Write down one memory
of this place that you'd like to
incorporate into your décor:*

THEME NAME

TAME ››› WILD!

NEUTRAL ››› COLORFUL

EASY ››› DIFFICULT

SIGNATURE DRINK

COLOR SCHEME

STATEMENT DÉCOR

PLAYLIST

ACKNOWLEDGMENTS

My mom, Nikki—my incredible role model and bestie who has inspired my imagination since I was a little girl, you have taught me to never stop believing in my dreams and to never stop creating. You have always reminded me that there is no limit to what I can achieve by just being me and letting my authentic self shine through, no matter how over-the-top I might be at times.

My dad, Rob—a man who not only is my best friend but has taught me the true meaning of being a strong woman and always believing in myself. Who has always taught me in life to never chase money but to always chase success! To always do everything to the best of my ability.

My brother, Greg—my rock and massive supporter who has been on the other end of every single phone call whenever I've doubted myself. Who has pushed me to continue on my own path even when I was unsure of the direction. Who guided me to get back on track and to level up when I started to lose sight of my end goal. A true inspiration in the entrepreneurial sphere.

My little sister, Steph—the young lady who is the epitome of kindness! She has been my sounding board and my adviser on many things throughout my life. She has helped me to see the best in every situation, good or bad. And helped me to let go of things that no longer serve me so that I can put my full energy into things that do! Her wisdom has helped me more than she even knows!

A and Papa, Grandma and Grandpa—thank you for always watching over me and motivating me to make you all proud!

Jamie—Wakeupwithjamie, thank you for always being a badass inspiration!

Captain Sandy—thanks for always being an inspiration and a fabulous supporter! You have truly always believed in me, and for that I am so grateful!

Marissa—Pumpkin! What can I say, it's been one hell of a journey! From our first meet and greet to diving headfirst into my book, it's been wild. Thank you for taking the leap of faith and believing in not only me but my vision! I would not be where I am today and my book would not exist without you. Thanks for being the boss-ass business big sister I never had. And thanks to Benny for introducing us and to Billy for setting it all up!

My Big Grand Cay family—Rob, Beryl, Herbie, Big A, Boy, Herbert, Nardo, Francis, Kenny, Tony, Jerry, Cookie, Sandra, and everyone else who inspired me from Little Grand Cay.

My closest friends, who have always been by my side and always believed in and put up with my crazy ideas—Jen, Lisa, Jaidles, Chintz, Kim, Dave, Alex, Brian, Mark, Ross, Soph, and Bleu. I love you and thank you all for being a part of my journey and life.

Cline family and friends—Tanner, Candice, Graham, Logan, Kait, Kelly, beautiful angel Kami, JR, Joycey, Sheila, Uncle Steve, and Mr. Jude! Thank you for accepting this little South African into your world of parties.

Lex—thanks for being the most fantastic photographer and making my vision burst into life through the lens!

Tash—thanks for making me feel and look absolutely fabulous! For the brilliant hair and makeup and the savage style!

Daniel—thanks for the festive fun and the sensational cover shot!

Harry—for supporting my vision and allowing me the time to bring it all to life!

The incredible Girl Friday Productions team—Kristin, Leah, Emilie, Rachel, Micah, and Dave—who put this magical book together. You took my vision and ideas and made them into more than I ever could have imagined! I'm blown away. Thank you!

Thank you to the following locations—Bodega Taqueria y Tequila, Byblos, Carillon Hotel, Dolce Italian Miami @ The Gale Hotel, Pizza Bar, Stiltsville Fish Bar, Joia Beach, Malibu Farms, Strip Steak by Michael Mina @ The Fontainbleau Hotel, Shelbourne Hotel.

Thanks also to—Alchemy Agency (Matt and team!), Boca Bargoons (Thanks Fran!!), HomeGoods, Jet Fresh Flowers, Michael's, Odd Balls Thrifty, Party City, Target.

ABOUT THE AUTHOR

The self-professed Queen of Theme, Christine "Bugsy" Drake is widely known for her role as a stew on Bravo's *Below Deck Mediterranean*, seasons 2 and 5, where her gorgeous signature tablescapes and over-the-top theme parties are often the star of the show. Born and raised in South Africa, she is a seasoned yachtie who began her career in floating hospitality in 2013. She has since worked on a private island in the Bahamas and sailed the seas on some of the world's most exclusive luxury yachts. Called "perhaps the greatest tablescape artist who has ever lived" by the *New York Times*, Bugsy always brings her passion and talent for stunning décor to the table.